FIFTH GRADE TECHNOLOGY

32 LESSONS EVERY FIFTH GRADER
CAN ACCOMPLISH ON A COMPUTER

FOURTH EDITION

Part Six of the Technology Curriculum by

Structured Learning

Fourth Edition 2011
Part Six of Structured Learning's Technology Curriculum
Visit the companion website at http://askatechteacher.com for more resources to teach
technology to children and online assistance with this textbook.

To receive free weekly digital technology tips and/or websites, send an email to
admin@structuredlearning.net with the message "Subscribe to Weekly Tips" or "Subscribe to
Weekly Websites"

ISBN 0-9787800-5-1

Printed in the United States of America

Introduction

This Structured Learning Technology Curriculum is designed to guide you and your child through a progressive growth of age-appropriate activities, resulting in a thorough knowledge of technology appropriate to your child's age level. If you didn't start with Kindergarten, go back and start there—even if your child is in Fifth grade. There are skills taught there that aren't covered here, because it is assumed your child already learned them.

This Fifth Grade Textbook is aligned with National Educational Technology Standards for Students (see Appendix) to insure your child receives the broadest educational training available. It is based on a time-proven method successfully used and honed in classrooms. It requires a commitment of forty-five minutes a week of uninterrupted concentration on computers, followed up with two sessions of fifteen minutes each spread out throughout the week to practice keyboarding (see Appendix). If you can give more that's great! If your time doesn't allow that as so many busy families don't, your child will still accomplish every goal within this book. The only rejoinder is: If there is a skill that your child doesn't get, spend some additional time reinforcing and reminding. S/he won't get every skill the first time, but when you see it come up a second or third time through the course of these workbooks, then it's time to concentrate. Some skills are more difficult than others for some students. It doesn't mean your child can't accomplish it. It just means they need a bit of extra work.

> "The problem with computers is they do what you tell them." — *Unknown.*

The purpose of this textbook is not to teach the step-by-step details of the myriad computer skills. There are many fine books that will explain how to add Word borders, put a text box in Publisher, shade the cells in Excel and create a blog. What those books don't tell you is when your child is old enough to comprehend the skills they are teaching. That is what we do here: Guide you toward providing the right information at the right time, which allows your child the best opportunity to succeed. Just as most children can't learn to read at two, or write at four, they shouldn't be introduced to the fine motor skills of speed typing in kindergarten. We make sure your child gets what s/he needs, at the right age. The end result is a phenomenal amount of learning in a short period of time.

If there are skills that you don't know how to show your child that aren't 'taught' in this book, and you can't find books that address those in the manner you seek, you can visit the blog (AskATechTeacher.wordpress.com), the wiki and the internet start page that accompany this book (see publisher's website for more information). You'll find lots of help there.

Programs Required for K-5

Take a look at the list of programs we use. Some are free downloads (click links) or have free alternatives. The focus is programs that can collaborate with school projects, will teach critical skills, and can be used throughout the student's educational career. Here are the minimum requirements. Free alternatives are noted with links. If you don't have a pdf of this book, contact the publisher for a discounted copy:

General	(K-2)	Intermediate (3-5)
Outlook (or free Gmail)	*KidPix (or free TuxPaint)*	*MS Office (or free Open Office, Google Docs)*
Google Earth (free dl)	*Type to Learn Jr. or*	*MS Publisher*
Internet browser	*free online keyboarding*	*Adobe Photoshop (or free Gimp)*
	MS Office	*Type to Learn (or free online keyboarding)*
	MS Publisher	*Oregon Trail (free online as classic edition)*

Here's an overview of topics covered, as well as which grade. It tells you the topic, but not the skills—that comes later in this introduction. Some are covered every year, which means they are critical skills that don't go away and change with time. Some are learned early. These, once mastered, are not revisited, like mouse skills. After the addition of the second button and the scroll, not much changes with mouse skills.

	Mouse Skills	Vocabulary And Hardware	Problem-solving	Windows and the Basics	Keyboard and shortcuts	Adobe Photoshop	Word	PowerPoint	Publisher	Excel	Google Earth	E-Mail	Graphics
K	☺	☺	☺	☺	☺								☺
1	☺	☺	☺	☺	☺				☺		☺		☺
2		☺	☺	☺	☺		☺	☺	☺		☺		☺
3		☺	☺	☺	☺		☺	☺	☺	☺	☺	☺	
4		☺	☺		☺		☺	☺	☺	☺	☺	☺	☺
5		☺	☺		☺	☺	☺		☺	☺	☺	☺	☺

Technology in general, and this curriculum specifically, builds on itself. What you learn a prior year will be used as you progress through the next grade level. For example, your child may have difficulty accomplishing the lessons laid out for fourth graders—say, typing 25 wpm with speed and accuracy—without going through those designated for grades K-3 sequentially. Have no fear, though: By the end of fifth grade, after following this series of lessons, they will accomplish everything necessary for Middle School.

Typical 45-minute Lesson

As you face a room full of eager faces, remember that you are a guide, not an autocrat. Use the Socratic Method—don't take over the student's mouse and click for them or type in a web address when they need to learn that skill. Even if it takes longer, guide them to the answer so they aren't afraid of how they got there. If you've been doing this since kindergarten, you know it works. In fact, by the end of kindergarten, you saw remarkable results.

When talking with students, always use the correct vocabulary. That's why I've included it on the lesson plan. Be sure to emphasize the vocabulary and expect students to understand it. Try the Vocabulary Board during one of the quarters/trimesters. Students love it and it highlights why they want to understand 'Geek Speak'.

Here's how I run a class:

- Students enter the room. They know to check the 'To Do' list on the overhead screen or Smart Board as they take their seats and plug their flash drive in. You're finishing up an email, but it doesn't matter. The beginning of class is student-directed.
- Students start with 10 minutes of typing practice, either using installed software or an online keyboarding program. Some days, they are directed to work on their site words in www.spellingcity.com or another active learning process that is self-directed.
- Next, there are three presentations (from *Google Earth Board, Problem-solving Board*, or *Vocabulary Board*). These rotate throughout the year, one per trimester/quarter. Students have selected their topic and presentation date. Whoever is up for the day will teach the class and take questions from the audience. This takes ten-twelve minutes. This week it's exploring the world with Google Earth.
- If it's the beginning of a month, I review assigned homework and take questions. If it's the end of a trimester, I review which skills have been accomplished during the last three months.
- If we are starting a new project in our year of project-based learning, I review it with them, take questions and we start. If they are in the middle of one, they use the balance of the class to work towards its completion. I monitor activities, answer questions, help where needed. They have access to installed software and the internet which makes this portion of class student-centered learning requiring critical thinking and problem-solving skills

- During their work, students are free to post vocabulary words they don't understand on the vocabulary board and problem-solving ideas on that board.
- Students who have completed the current project take advantage of 'sponge activities' from a topic of their choice, practice keyboarding for the upcoming speed quiz or help a classmate struggling with a prickly skill. I include a variety of topical websites on a class internet start page (see inset for sample). Students know any websites on this page can be used by them during sponge time.
- Students who finish early may also access the class wiki (see inset for sample) to see what they might have missed in earlier classes.

How to Achieve Your Goals on a Weekly Basis

Here's how to be sure your child gets the most out of the time s/he spends on their technology education:

☐ Set aside 45 minutes for the core lesson and 15 minutes twice more during the week to reinforce.

☐ Sit straight with body centered in front of keyboard, legs in front of body, elbows at his/her sides.

☐ Place both hands in home-row position even though they use only one hand at a time. Let the other rest in home position waiting for its turn.

☐ Set book to left of keyboard—never in front of monitor.

☐ Remember: Parent/teacher is the guide—not the doer!

☐ Don't be distracted.

☐ Don't blame the computer. Always take responsibility.

☐ Save early. Save often.

☐ Always make a back-up of work.

☐ Use tech vocabulary during lesson.

☐ Once a problem solution is introduced (i.e., *what's today's date*), have the student do it the next time—don't do it for them!

☐ Check off each lesson item as the student accomplishes it.

1. When computing, whatever happens, behave as though you meant it to happen.
2. He who laughs last probably made a back-up.
3. If at first you don't succeed, blame your computer.
4. A complex system that does not work is invariably found to have evolved from a simpler system that worked just fine.
5. A computer program will always do what you tell it to do, but rarely what you want to do.

— *Murphy's Laws of Computing*

Table of Contents

K-5 TECHNOLOGY SCOPE AND SEQUENCE

Check each skill off with I/W/M/C under '5' as student accomplishes it
(Column 1 refers to the ISTE Standard addressed by the skill)

I=Introduced W=Working on M=Mastered C=Connected to Classwork

ISTE			K	1	2	3	4	5
I	**Care and Use of the Computer**							
		Learn and practice safety on the Internet	I	W	W	W	M	C
		Keep your body to yourself—don't touch neighbor's kb	I	W	W	W	M	C
		Internet security—what it means, why	I	I	I	W	M	C
		Use of network file folders to save personal work	I	I	W	W	M	C
II	**Computer Hardware**							
		Understand how parts of the computer connect	I	W	M	C	C	C
		Know the names of all computer hardware	I	W	M	C	C	C
		Know how to adjust volume	I	W	M	C	C	C
		Know how to use the keyboard, mouse	I	W	M	C	C	C
		Know all parts of keyboard—Alt, F-row, space bar, etc.	I	W	M	C	C	C
		Know how to turn monitor on/off	I	W	M	C	C	C
		Know how to power computer on, off	I	W	M	C	C	C
III	**Basic Computer Skills**							
		Know how to add file folders						I
		Know basic computer vocab—hardware and skills		I	W	M	C	C
		Understand Windows—desktop, icons, start button, etc.			I	W	M	C
		Understand the Ctr+Alt+Del, use of Task Manager				I	W	M
		Know how to drag-drop from one window to another						I
		Know how to log-on				I	W	M	C
		Know how to create a macro (for MLA heading)						I
		Understand mouse skills	I	W	M	C	C	C
		Understand right-click menus				I	W	M	C
		Know how to Open/Save/close a document, save-as, print	I	W	M	C	C	C
		Know how to solve common problems	I	W	M	C	C	C
		Know how to problem-solve with help files						I
		Understand tool bars in Word, Publisher, etc.					I	W	M
		Know how to use flash drives—USB port, save-to, etc.					I	W	M
		Know how to use program you haven't been taught					I	W	M
		Know how to create wallpaper					I	W	M
		Understand differences/similarities between programs					I	W	M
IV	**Typing and Word Processing**							
	KB							
		Achieve age-appropriate speed and accuracy					I	W	M

		Know Alt, Ctrl, Backspace, spacebar, enter, tab, shift etc.	I	W	M	C	C	C
		Know when to use cap key	I	W	M	C	C	C
		Know how to compose at keyboard		I	W	M	C	C
		Know correct spacing after words, sentences, paragraphs		I	W	M	C	C
		Use correct keyboarding posture	I	W	M	C	C	C
		Know how to use exclamation and question mark			I	W	M	C
		Understand F row				I	W	M
		Follow grammar/spelling rules	I	W	M	C	C	C
		Know when to use delete, backspace	I	W	M	C	C	C
		Know and use common keyboard shortcuts	I	W	M	C	C	C
		Know to put cursor in specific location, i.e., for graphic			I	W	M	C
		Be able to use online keyboarding sites			I	W	M	C
	WP							
		Understand Word basics			I	W	M	C
		Know how to move text within document					I	W
		Know how to use Ctrl+Enter to force a new page			I	W	M	C
		Know how to add a header/footer to a document			I	W	M	C
		Know how to format a document—fonts, borders, etc.			I	W	M	C
		Know how to use spell-check and grammar-check			I	W	M	C
		Know how to use word wrap				I	W	M
		Know how to insert pictures from clipart, file pic, internet			I	W	M	C
		Know how to insert tables				I	W	M
		Know how to insert text box						I
		Know how to create graphic organizers			I	W	M	C
		Know how to insert headers and footers			I	W	M	C
		Know how to create bullet lists and numbered lists					I	W
		Know how to outline						I
		Know print with print preview			I	W	M	C
		Know how to create and use an embedded link					I	W
		Understand Word pad, Notepad						I
V	**Designing (Photo, video, document)**							
		Introduce Digital cameras	I	I	I	I	I	I
		Know how to draw in one program and insert into another				I	W	M	C
		Insert geometric shapes into KidPix	I	W	W			
	Publisher							
		Know how to plan a publication			I	W	M	C
		Identify and understand parts of Publisher screen			I	W	M	C
		Know how to use tools, toolbars in Publisher			I	W	M	C
		Know how to add/edit text using the text box			I	W	M	C
		Know how to resize/move graphics			I	W	M	C
		Know how to use font schemes			I	W	M	C

	Skill						
	Know how to use color schemes			I	W	M	C
	Know how to add/delete a page, a picture or text				I	W	M
	Know how to insert a Table of Contents				I	W	M
	Know how to insert footer				I	W	M
	Know how to make a Card			I	W	M	C
	Know how to make a flier			I	W	M	C
	Know how to make a cover page				I	W	M
	Know how to make a simple storybook				I	W	M
	Know how to make a newsletter						I
	Know how to make a trifold brochure				I	W	M
	Know how to make a calendar						I

Photoshop

	Skill						
	Know how to plan a project						I
	Identify and understand the parts of the Photoshop screen						I
	Know how to use tools, toolbars in Photoshop						I
	Know how to add/edit text using the text box						I
	Know how to insert pictures (from clip art, file folder)						I
	Know how to use artistic renderings						I
	Know how to use auto fixes						I
	Know how to clone in a pic and across pictures						I
	Know how to crop with marquee, lasso tool, magic wand						I
	Know how to reset screen to default						I
	Know how to use history to go back in time						I
	Understand the use of 'layers' in constructing a project						I
	Know how to use the healing brush tool						I
	Know how to use filters						I
	Know how to replace backgrounds in pictures						I
	Know how to use 'Actions' tool on tool bar						I
	Know how to use art history brush						I
	Know how to use the paint brush						I

VI Presenting

	Skill						
	Introduce PowerPoint			I	W	M	C
	Understand layout, screen, tools, toolbars, placesavers			I	W	M	C
	Know how to insert text, edit, format			I	W	M	C
	Know how to insert pictures from file, internet, clip-art			I	W	M	C
	Understand how to add backgrounds to one or all slides			I	W	M	C
	Know how to insert animated GIF's/short movies			I	W	M	C
	Know how to insert animation into slides			I	W	M	C
	Know how to add transitions between slides			I	W	M	C
	Know how to add custom animations to slides			I	W	M	C
	Practice presentation skills			I	W	M	C
	Know how to have slides automatically			I	W	M	C
	Know how to insert interactive hyperlinks					I	W

		Know how to add/rearrange slides				I	W	M	C
		Know how to add music and sounds to one slide or many						I	W
		Understand and practice presentation skills				I	W	M	C
VII	**Spreadsheets**								
		Understand the layout, screen, tools, toolbars					I	W	M
		Know how to sort data					I	W	M
		Know how to format data					I	W	M
		Know how to use basic formulas					I	W	M
		Know how to recolor tabs and rename tabs					I	W	M
		Know how to widen columns and rows					I	W	M
		Know how to enter data and make a quick graph					I	W	M
		Know how to label x and y axis on graphs					I	W	M
		Know how to format a chart					I	W	M
		Know how to add a hyperlink to spreadsheet							I
		Know how to use print preview					I	W	M
		Know how to add headers/footers							I
VIII	**Internet basics**								
		Understand elements of an Internet address/URL				I	W	M	C
		Understand use of a start page		I	W	M	C	C	C
		Understand use of forward/back buttons, home, links			I	W	M	C	C
		Know how to use Bookmarks			I	W	M	C	C
		Understand difference between search and address bars		I	W	M	C	C	C
		Know how to use scroll bars		I	W	M	C	C	C
		Know how to save images and ethical considerations		I	W	M	C	C	C
		Know how to use the right click					I	W	M
		Know how to search and research on Google					I	W	M
		Know how to identify reliable sources on the internet					I	W	M
		Understand how to evaluate and identify reliable websites					I	W	M
	Web 2.0								
		Learn how to check grades online							I
		Understand Cloud computing (create a logo, avatar, etc.)					I	W	M
		Understand blogs and how to participate in them							1
		Understand an Internet start page and how to use it		I	W	M	C	C	C
		Understand internet Netiquette					I	W	M
		Understand class webpages, share info, upload files, etc.					I	W	M
IX	**Integrated — Multi-media**								
		Know how to follow directions in the use of computers		I	W	M	C	C	C
		Understand digital camera		I	W	M	C	C	C
		Know how to mix words and pictures to communicate		I	W	M	C	C	C

	Google Earth						
	Know how to find a location on Google Earth	I	W	M	C	C	C
	Know how to add a location to Google Earth's 'Places'				I	W	M
	Understand the use of latitudes and longitudes				I	W	M
	Know how to play a tour	I	W	M	C	C	C
	Know how to create a tour					I	W
	Know how to use Google Earth Community						I
	Know how to use the ruler to measure distances						I
	Email						
	Know how to email homework to teachers				I	W	M
	Understand parts of an email—subject, to, cc, message				I	W	M
	Understand and use proper email etiquette				I	W	M
	Understand the use of cc in an email				I	W	M
	Know how to attach a document to an email				I	W	M

Lesson #1—Introduction

Vocabulary	Problem solving	Collaborations
▓ *AVI* ▓ *Digital* ▓ *Multimedia* ▓ *Right-mouse button* ▓ *Right-click menu* ▓ *Windows* ▓ *Back-up* ▓ *PC*	▓ *What if double-click doesn't work (push enter)* ▓ *What if monitor doesn't work (check the power)* ▓ *What if volume doesn't work (check the control)* ▓ *What if computer doesn't work (check the power)*	*"To go forward, you must back up."* *—Cardinal rule of computing*
NETS-S Standards *5. Digital Citizenship, 6. Technology Concepts*		

Lesson questions? Go to http://askatechteacher.com

Review rules—tour classroom
_____ No excuses
_____ Don't blame people; don't blame the computer
_____ Save early, save often
_____ No food or drink around computer
_____ Respect the work of others and yourself

Review homework policy
_____ Homework is in the back of this workbook, due via email
Homework due monthly, last day of month

Review Hardware
_____ Mouse buttons—left and right, double click, scroll in center
_____ CPU—power button, CD drive, USB port
_____ Monitor—power button, screen, station number
_____ Headphones—volume slider, size adjustment
_____ Keyboard—home row, F4, enter, spacebar, Ctrl, alt, shift
_____ Review how parts connect—behind CPU, under table, in front ports

Review 'save' and 'save-as' rules on next pages; review how to delete ('delete' key and backspace)

Take digital picture and AVI movie; Discuss digital; Discuss multimedia

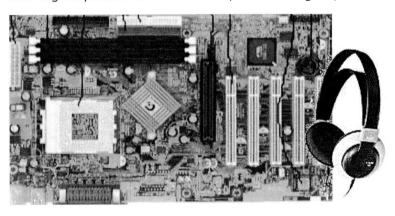

NAME THE PARTS OF THE COMPUTER

WHAT'S THE DIFFERENCE BETWEEN SAVE AND SAVE AS?

SAVE

- Save the first time
- Resave changes to the same location

SAVE AS

- Resave under a new name
- Resave to a new location

Difference between 'Backspace' and 'Delete'

Put this on the wall of your classroom/lab

TWO WAYS

TO DELETE

BACKSPACE

DELETE

Deletes to the left, one character at a time

Deletes to the right, one character at a time

Lesson #2—Computer Hardware

Vocabulary	Problem solving	Collaborations
Escape *Icon* *Desktop* *Macro* *Protocol* *Ctrl* *Shortkey*	*My mouse doesn't work (wake it up)* *My volume doesn't work (check the control)* *Double-click doesn't work (push enter)* *My computer doesn't work (check power, move mouse)* *Where's the right mouse button?*	*Spelling* *Grammar* *Critical thinking*
NETS-S Standards *2. Communication; 5. Digital Citizenship; 6. Technology Concepts*		

Lesson questions? Go to http://askatechteacher.com

Review parts of computer—quiz next week; graded on spelling; see guide on next pages

_____ All major parts (CPU, monitor, keyboard, mouse, headphones, volume, printer, power)

Speed quiz today (see samples on next pages)—remember how this was done in 3rd/4th gr[a]

_____ Warm up with Type to Learn or online keyboarding program (see appendix for examples)

_____ Don't look at the keys; fingers on home row; elbows at your sides

_____ Open Word for speed quiz; teach students how to create a macro for heading; use Ctrl+Alt+H for macro (this one doesn't invoke any other macro)

_____ 5-minute speed quiz, one-minute spell-check at end; type word count at bottom

_____ Goals: 30 wpm by end of 5th grade (see details on next pages)

_____ Save to network file folder; Print (use shortkey Ctrl+P)

_____ Review important keys students should know on the keyboard (see next pages)

Review Homework Policy—due monthly via email (if possible),

_____ File name protocol 'lastname 5 HW#'

_____ Homework #1 and #2 due end of month—take questions

Review online access to digital lockers; show students how to upload to theirs. Have them practice by uploading the Hardware Study Guide from What We did Today on class webpage (click link for sample) to their digital lockers for study for next week

HARDWARE—PARTS OF THE COMPUTER

Name each part of the computer hardware system on the line next to it and label it as an 'input' device or an 'output' device.

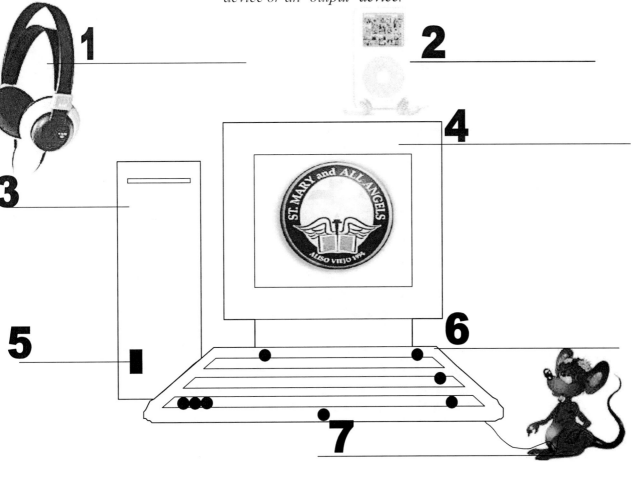

1 _____

2 _____

3 _____

4 _____

5 _____

6 _____

7 _____

Word Bank:

Headphones	*Mouse*	*USB Port*
Keyboard	*Peripheral*	
Monitor	*Tower/CPU*	

Label the keys with a circle ⬤ over them. Use this word bank:

Ctrl	*Spacebar*	*Shift*
Alt	*Flying Windows*	*Enter*
Backspace	*F4*	

Sample Keyboard Speed Quiz

The Best Thing In The World

Once upon a time, four princes lived in a far away land. Their father was old. One day he said, "I will not live long now. Today you start out into the world. In a year, bring back the best thing you have found. The one who can pick the best thing shall be my new king."

The first brother said he would look in every city or town to buy the best thing for his father." The next two brothers said they would both go on fast ships over the sea to find something better.

The last brother said, "I am going to ask the people here in our own land to tell me the best thing." The other three began to laugh. "Then you will never be king!" The last brother started off. When he had gone about six miles, he met a man. "What do you carry in those big bags?" he asked. "The best thing in the world," said the man. "These are full of good nuts which fall from my five trees."

"I don't think that would work," said the brother to himself, "I must try again."

He went another seven miles and found a small brown bird. It had been hurt, so he put it in his coat where it could keep warm. As he went on, he saw a girl crying. He ran to meet her.

"Why are you crying?" he asked the little girl.

"I want to get some water from the well," she said. "We use so much. We drink cold water. We wash the clothes clean with hot water. But I do not know how to pull it up. Please show me."

The brother said, "Hold this bird and I will help you. It does not fly around anymore because it got its wing hurt."

"Thank you. What a pretty bird! I wish you would give it to me. If you will let me keep it, I will always be very kind to it. I will take care of it myself and make it grow well."

"Yes, you may have it," said the brother.

So he gave her the bird and went on. At night, he went to sleep under a round yellow haystack. When it was light again he walked on. Every day he would walk eight or ten miles. He asked the people about the best thing in the world. Some said it was best to sing. Some said it was best to run and jump and play. Some said the green grasses were best. Some liked the red and blue and white flowers best. One man said the best thing was to ride a black horse. The Prince always stopped to help people who needed it. Soon he made many friends. All the people began to like him. They would say, "See there goes the king's son. He would be just the right kind of king for us."

Every door was open to him. The people would call to him to stop. They would ask him to come and eat with them. After he ate, he would sit down and read to the children. After he read, he showed them how to draw and write. Months went by. He still had no beautiful thing to take to his father. Just before the year was done, he went home again. The time came went he king called his sons together.

"What did you bring?" He asked them all. The other brothers had many beautiful things.
"And what did you bring?" said the king to the last brother.

"This is too funny!" said the other brothers. "He has nothing!"

But the king was kind to the last brother. "What did you bring me?" the king asked again.

"I bring only the friendship of your people," said the last the brother.

"That is the best thing!" cried his father. "You shall be the new king."

This passage contains all of the 220 Dolch Basic Sight Words. Adapted from http://www.bristolvaschools.org/mwarren/DolchWords.htm

Third-Fifth Grade Keyboarding Grading

By third grade, students are expected to use the good traits they've acquired in K-2 to improve keyboarding speed and accuracy. I give them a five-minute typing test once a trimester. They're graded on speed, accuracy, and good typing habits. As they type, I walk around and anecdotally judge their posture, hand position, use of fingers, etc. and deduct points if they are inadequate.

At the end of the five-minute quiz, I allow one minute to correct spelling errors using a right-click on the red squiggly lines.

Grading is based on improvement from their last quiz. A student who types 10 wpm could get a 7/10 if he didn't improve or a 10/10 if he improved from 8wom on the last quiz. Here's the breakdown:

20% improvement:	10/10
10% improvement:	9/10
1-10% improvement:	8/10
No improvement:	7/10
Slowed down:	6/10

I post a list of keyboard speedsters in each class on the bulletin board. I also post the winning class (fastest) for all to see. Students who reach the grade level standard for speed and accuracy get a free dress pass (we are a uniform school). This is quite exciting for them:

Grade level standards are:

K-2	None
3rd Grade:	15 wpm
4th Grade:	25 wpm
5th Grade:	30 wpm

KEYS YOU SHOULD KNOW

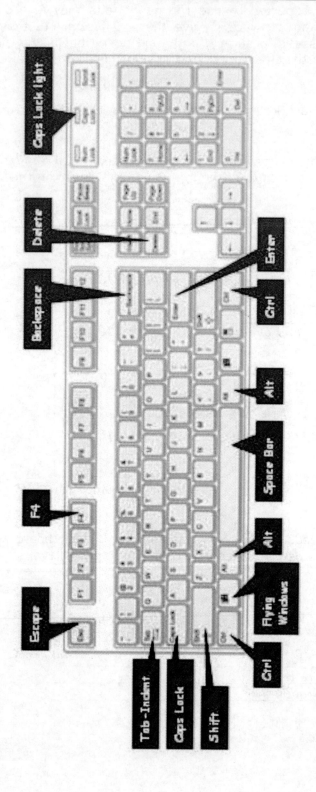

Assume the Position

- Legs centered in front of body
- Body centered in front of keyboard
- Hands curved over home row
- Document to left of computer
- Use right thumb for space bar
- Eyes on screen

Lesson #3—Celestia

Vocabulary	Problem solving	Collaborations
Alt *F4* *Etiquette* *Email* *Cc* *Urgent*	*My monitor doesn't work (check power button)* *How do I move between cells (tab)* *What's 'cc'? (send a copy of the email to someone else)* *How do I close a program (Alt+F4)*	*Grammar* *Spelling* *Science* *Astronomy*
NETS-S Standards *4. Problem solving; 6. Technology concepts*		

Lesson questions? Go to http://askatechteacher.com

Hardware Quiz—students can retake for a better grade if need be

_____ TTL4 when done (or go to an online typing site) while waiting on rest of class

Sign up for Problem Solving Board—starts next week (see next pages). Remember 3rd and 4th grade?

_____ Sign up for a problem to solve. Students can get the solution from family, friends, neighbors or even the teacher as a last resort. They are responsible for teaching their classmates how to solve the problem.

_____ Sign up for a date to present. They will tell their classmates a problem, how to solve it and take questions. It takes only about three minutes.

_____ Review how you'll grade them (see next pages)

_____ Students can sign up before/after school, lunch, any time they're free.

_____ Review Most Common Problems and shortkeys listed on following pages; encourage students to use these shortkeys as often as possible

Outlook—review sample email; have students complete but not send

_____ To, cc, subject line, body of email, attachment, urgent

_____ Review email etiquette; ask students to review this with parents also

_____ Homework is emailed when possible; student responsibility to spell address correctly, notice when the email 'bounces back', resend if necessary

Celestia—explore the Universe (free download from http://www.shatters.net/celestia/)

_____ Let students explore this beautiful program; run demo under Help-run demo

_____ Follow directions on study guide (see next pages)

Bring science book next week to outline a chapter

Problem Solving Board Sign-up

	Teacher #1	Teacher #2	Teacher #3
Week of October 2nd			
Week of October 9th			
Week of October 16th			
Week of October 23rd			
Week of October 30th			
Week of November 6th			
Week of November 13th			
Week of November 27th			

	Teacher #1	Teacher #2	Teacher #3
What if the double-click doesn't work			
What if the monitor doesn't work			
What if the volume doesn't work			
What if the computer doesn't work			
What if the mouse doesn't work			
What's the right-mouse button for?			
What keyboard shortcut closes program			
How do I move between cells/boxes?			
How do I figure out today's date?			
What if the capital doesn't work			
What if my toolbar disappears			
What if the document disappears			
Keyboard shortcut for 'undo'			
How do I search for a file			
What if the program disappears			
What if the program freezes			
What is the protocol for saving a file			
What is protocol for email subject line			
What does 'CC' mean in an email			
How do I exit a screen I'm stuck in			
How do I double space in Word			
How do I add a footer in Word			
How do I add a watermark in Word			
How do I make a macro in Word			
How do I add a border in Word			
How do I add a hyperlink in Word			
Keyboard shortcuts for B, I, U			

PROBLEM SOLVING BOARD
GRADING

Name: _____

Class: _____

Knew question   _____

Knew answer   _____

Asked audience for help if didn't know answer   _____

No umm's, stutters   _____

No nervous movements (giggles, wiggles, etc.)   _____

Overall   _____

Common problems students face with computers

	Problem	Solution
1	My browser is too small	*Double click the blue bar*
2.	Browser tool bar missing	*Push F11*
3.	Exit a program	*Alt+F4*
4.	Today's date	*Hover over clock* *Shift+Alt+D in Word*
5.	Double click doesn't work	*Push enter*
7.	Start button disappeared	*Use Windows button*
8.	Program disappeared	*Check taskbar*
9.	Erased my document	*Ctrl+Z*
10.	I can't find a tool	*Right click on screen; it'll show most common tools*
11.	My screen is frozen	*Clear a dialogue box* *Press Escape four times*
12.	My menu command is grey	*Press escape 4 times and try again*
13.	Can't find Bold, Italic, Underline	*Use Ctrl+B, Ctrl+I, Ctrl+U*

UNDO

is your

Friend

Popular shortkeys students love using

Maximize window	Double click title bar
Quick Exit	Alt+F4
Date and Time	Shift+Alt+D = Date
	Shift+Alt+T = Time
Show taskbar	WK (Windows key)
Shows desktop	WK+M

Ctrl Key Combinations

CTRL+C: Copy	CTRL+P: Print
CTRL+X: Cut	CTRL+K: Add hyperlink
CTRL+V: Paste	CTRL+E: Center align
CTRL+Z: Undo	CTRL+L: Left align
CTRL+B: Bold	CTRL+R: Right align
CTRL+U: Underline	CTRL+ : Zoom in Internet
CTRL+I: Italic	CTRL- : Zoom out Internet

Fun Keyboard Shortcuts:

‹ + = + › = ⇔

— + › = →

: +) = ☺

Add Your Favorite:

EMAIL ETIQUETTE

1. Use proper formatting, spelling, grammar

2. CC anyone you mention

3. Subject line is a quick summary of what your email discusses

4. Use correct subject line protocol—lastname-grade-topic (lastname3hw2)

5. Answer received emails swiftly

6. Re-read your email before sending

7. Don't use capitals—THIS IS SHOUTING

8. Don't leave out the subject line

9. Don't attach unnecessary files

10. Don't overuse the high priority

11. Don't email confidential information

12. Don't email offensive remarks

13. Don't forward chain letters or spam

14. Don't open attachments from strangers

<u>CELESTIA 'TO DO' LIST</u>

- o **Go to 'Help-run demo'**
- o **Go to 'navigation-tour guide'**
- o **Go to 'navigation-solar system browser'**
- o **Go to 'navigation-star browser'**
- o **Go to Google Earth, select solar system**

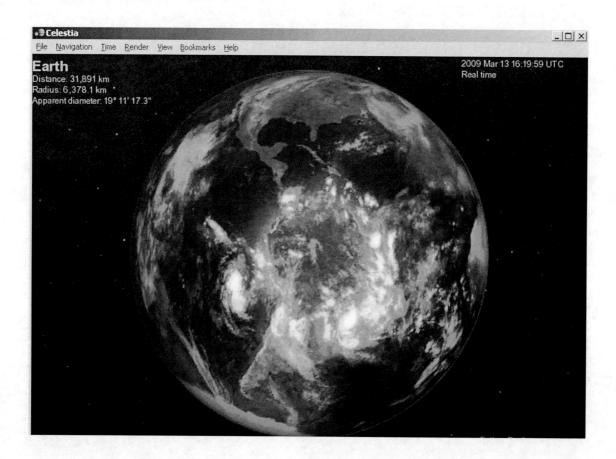

Lesson #4—Outlining in Word

Vocabulary	Problem solving	Collaborations
▪ *back space* ▪ *escape* ▪ *heading* ▪ *alignment* ▪ *outline* ▪ *indent* ▪ *icons* ▪ *ribbon* ▪ *log on*	▪ *Capital doesn't work (Is Caps Lock key on?)* ▪ *What is today's date (hover over clock in lower right corner or push Shift+Alt+D)* ▪ *How do I exit a program (Alt+F4)*	▪ *Science* ▪ *Grammar* ▪ *Spelling* ▪ *Outlining*

NETS-S Standards
6. Technology operations and concepts

Lesson questions? Go to http://askatechteacher.com

Type to Learn 4 or online keyboarding program (see appendix)

_____ Homework due end of month—Any questions on homework or how to email?

If student didn't do as well as hoped on Hardware quiz, retake it for full credit

Problem Solving Board starts today— Be encouraging; for some, this is difficult.

Lesson plan: Outlining in MS Word—Review with students how to outline using Word's ridiculously simple outline tools (numbered list, tab and shift+tab). Remember how this was done in 4ᵗʰ grade. Students can use any class textbook or notes (we'll use science today). Help them get started, and then let them figure it out themselves.

_____ Review MS Word menu bar, ribbons

_____ Put heading—left-aligned—at top of page: student name, teacher, date

_____ Put title on page: centered, underlined (use tools on ribbon)

_____ To outline in Word, use two ribbon tools: numbered list tool, decrease/increase indent (see inset below)

_____ Or, use keyboard short cuts: tab (increase indent), shift+tab (decrease)

_____ Enter text; push enter to go to next number; Word automatically adds the next number; decide if text indent must increase or decreased

_____ If you get out of outline, backspace to last entry, and 'enter'

_____ Close down to desktop using Alt+F4

Your name
Your teacher
Date (shift+alt+D)

CLIMATES AND HOW THEY CHANGE

1. Climate
   a. Climate
   b. Microclimate
2. Climate and Location
3. World Climates
   a. Polar zone
   b. Mountain zone

1. Bullet or #'d list

2. indent or exdent

OUTLINING

CLIMATES AND HOW THEY CHANGE

1. Climate
   a. Temperature
   b. Humidity
   c. Atmospheric pressure
   d. Wind rain
2. World Climates
   a. Polar zone
   b. Mountain zone
   c. Temperate zone
   d. Tropical zone
   e. Desert zone
3. Climate changes
   a. El Nino
   b. Ice age
4. Human effect on climate
   a. Greenhouse effect
   b. Global warming
   c. Seeding clouds

Lesson #5—Introduction to Google Earth

Vocabulary	Problem solving	Collaborations
▪ *Font* ▪ *Alignment* ▪ *Wallpaper* ▪ *Screen* ▪ *Task bar* ▪ *Format*	▪ *I can't close down (Alt+F4)* ▪ *My document disappeared (Ctrl+Z)* ▪ *I can't find my file (Start-Search)*	▪ *Grammar* ▪ *Spelling* ▪ *Science* ▪ *Geography*
NETS-S Standards *2. Communication; 6. Technology operations*		

Lesson questions? Go to http://askatechteacher.com

Type to Learn 4 or online keyboarding program (see appendix)

_____ Correct posture, elbows at side, hand position, legs in front of body

Problem solving board—continue with presentations

Lesson Plan: Google Earth—Locate the major latitudes and longitudes on Google Earth. Locate countries along the same latitude/longitude. Zoom in to see how exact lats and longs get. Students also find their own house by lat and long. Give students a lat and long and see if they can figure out where it is on the globe

_____ Open Google Earth. Find 'view', 'grid' to activate lats and longs. Remember skills learned in 2nd, 3rd, 4th grade.

_____ Have students locate two countries on each latitude. Use Placemark tool (yellow push pin) to secure the location of each. Measure the distance between the two countries using the Google Earth ruler. It doesn't have to be exact. Just measure from within one country to within another. Student answers will be slightly different, but they'll be surprised at the miles between their choices (see inset below and see sample answer on worksheet on next page).

_____ Complete sheet (see next page) online with partner. Submit to drop box/email.

Extra: Make wallpaper for computer desktop. Remember 3rd grade? Five ways to do this:

_____ One: Right click on Desktop; Select 'personalize', 'desktop background' and pick one.

_____ Two: Go to 'Pictures' folder on computer; right click on one you like and 'set as background'

_____ Three: Go to wallpaper website and download one. Try National Geographic.

_____ Four: Go to internet; right click on a picture and 'set as desktop background'

_____ Five: Create your own in KidPix (or Paint).

"A computer does what you tell it to do, not what you want it to do."

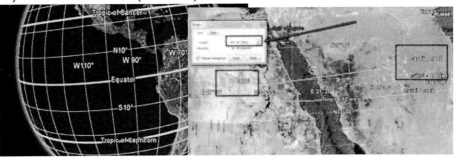

GOOGLE EARTH LATITUDE/LONGITUDES

Name: _____

Teacher: _____

Find two countries that each of the major lats and longs (latitudes and longitudes) go through and note the distance between them:

1. Tropic of Cancer—Distance between countries: 1002 miles___
    a. _Egypt_
    b. _Saudi Arabia_
2. Arctic Circle_____
    a.
    b.
3. Tropic of Capricorn_____
    a.
    b.
4. Antarctic Circle_____
    a.
    b.
5. Prime meridian_____
    a.
    b.
6. International date line_____
    a.
    b.
7. Equator _____
    a.
    b.

Lesson #6—Graphic Organizers

Vocabulary	Problem solving	Collaborations
☐ Right-click ☐ Desktop ☐ Background ☐ Graphic organizer ☐ Table ☐ Diagram	☐ What if log-on doesn't work? ☐ How do I open a program ☐ How do I close a program ☐ Log-on name ☐ Log-on password	☐ Science ☐ Graphic design
NETS-S Standards 2. Communication; 4. Problem solving; 6. Technology operations		

Lesson questions? Go to http://askatechteacher.com

Type to Learn or online typing program
_____ Good posture, hand position, body position, elbows at sides
Problem solving board—continue with presentations

Lesson Plan: Animal adaptations organized in MS Word—This is a great project that mixes the visual with the written. Students loved collaborating to come up with the adaptations that allowed the animal to thrive in a particular environ. Overall a popular project that teaches a lot. Easily completed in 30 minutes.

_____ Open MS Word. Add heading (name, teacher, date using Shift+Alt+D shortkey)
_____ Insert MS Word Organizational SmartArt—Hierarchy.
_____ Add 'Animal Adaptations as the first tier. Bold the title, underline—make it stand out
_____ Turn page from 'portrait' to 'landscape'. Discuss what this means.
_____ Have students suggest adaptations that have allowed animals to survive environmental changes. See the ones suggested in sample (next pages). Show students how to add shapes, how to make sure they are linked to the top level
_____ Add shapes so there are six under the main level *Animal Adaptations*
_____ Students fill six adaptations that allowed animals to survive in varying habitats. Have students discuss this with neighbors to come up with enough. Think what they've covered in the classroom. Jog their memory if necessary to the unique characteristics that certain animals have. Are claws useful in surviving? What about feathers—how would those make an animal more suited to an environ?
_____ Once adaptations are completed, students add a shape under each
_____ Now, students find an animal that has that characteristic using Google images. Copy-paste that animal into the shape and resize to fit. I suggest the thumbnail–it fits with minimal resizing. Plus, it serves as a link for future research (hover over image to see link)
_____ Allow students ample time to explore the plethora of amazing animal pictures that represent the adaptations they selected.
_____ Use ribbon tools to color diagram to taste. Save and print.
_____ Extra: Create a table to convey the same information in a different way. This is done independently because students have created many tables in 2nd, 3rd and 4th grade.
_____ Print preview to be sure everything fits on one page; save and print

Name

Date

Teacher

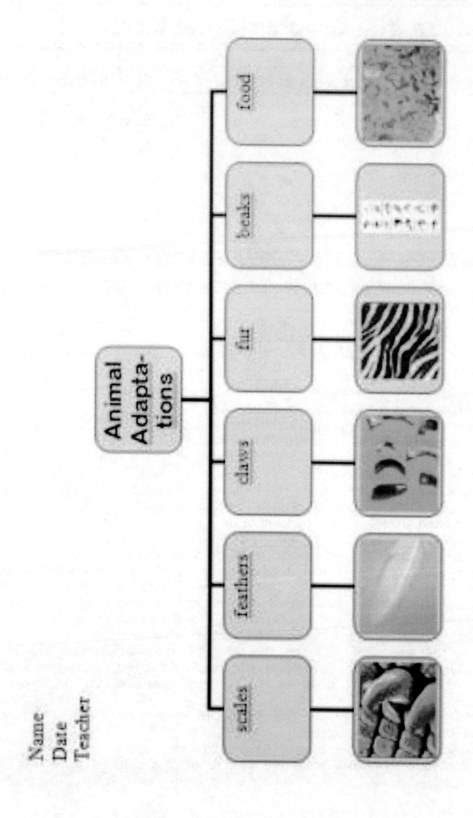

Animal Adaptations

- food
- beaks
- fur
- claws
- feathers
- scales

7 MS Word Tricks Every Teacher Should Know

The faster you teach students to be problem solvers, the more they'll learn. Computers are a foreign language. Even with small class sizes, the more students can do for themselves, the more fun they'll have learning the intricacies of technology.

The good news is, students love to be independent. They find it cool to know keyboard shortcuts for getting stuff done. In my class, students can help their neighbors, and they love showing off their problem solving skills. Here are 9 tricks that cover many common problems students will face using MS Word:

1. Ctrl+Z–undo
This will be your favorite. There are too many times to mention when I've had a frantic student, almost in tears because s/he thought s/he'd lost his/her document, and two seconds later I retrieved it. I was a hero for a class period.

2. Macro for a heading
This is great for students who have to remember MLA rules. What goes in a heading? How big are the margins? Where's a page number go? No worries. Create a macro and save the resulting document as a template. Never more worry.

3. How to find lost documents
It takes a while for users to get accustomed to saving files on a network. Often, documents end up lost (in my school, students must drill down through five levels to get to their unique location). My students learn early to use 'search' on the start menu.

4. How to insert data
The 'insert' key is so confusing I'm told it is being inactivated in the future. If students complain they lose data as they type, this is probably why. Show them how to push the 'insert' key and all will be fixed.

5. Show-hide tool.
Kids try to strong-arm Word into doing their will–often the wrong way. My favorite is 'enter enter' as a shortcut to double space. It seems to work until they have to edit the document, and then everything gets messed up. Have students push the **show-hide button** to see if they're using the double space tool. Then, show them where the icon is.

6. Tables—they work so much better than columns and tabs.
Teach it to kids **early and use it often**. It will save you miles of distress.

7. How to insert the date
It takes until Middle School for students to remember the date. Before that, they will always ask. Show them the **Shift+Alt+D** shortkey that inserts the current date into Word. They love it and it saves a lot of time for you.

Lesson #7—Introduction to Excel

Vocabulary	Problem solving	Collaborations
☐ *Mean* ☐ *Median* ☐ *Mode* ☐ *Average* ☐ *Formula* ☐ *Calculation*	☐ *What if program disappears (look on taskbar)?* ☐ *What is today's date?(Shift+Alt+D)* ☐ *I can't find my document/ file (Start-search)* ☐ *My right-click doesn't work (reboot)*	☐ *Math* ☐ *Problem-solving*

NETS-S Standards
1. Creativity and innovation; 4. Problem solving; 6. Technology operations

Lesson questions? Go to http://askatechteacher.com

TTL4 or online keyboard website—goal is 30 wpm by the end of 5th grade

_____ Correct posture, legs in front; hands on home row, curved over keys

Problem-solving Board—continue presentations

Lesson plan: MS Excel—evaluate data using Excel's formulas. Use data from the recent speed quiz or tie into a classroom discussion. What was the mean/median/mode for the class

_____ Review Excel basics—rows, columns, cells, naming protocol for cells (i.e., A1), ribbons, tools, worksheets, workbooks

_____ Rename the worksheet (tab) 'speed quiz'; color to preference (remember doing this in 3rd and 4th grade)

_____ Go to A1—add title (T2 Speed Quiz)

_____ Go to A2—add data (in words per minute) in a column; *enter* moves down column; *tab* moves to the next column; *shift+tab* moves to previous column. Display numbers on overhead or SmartBoard.

_____ Remind students: only put numbers in cells—Excel can't evaluate letters or symbols

_____ Discuss the meaning of mean, median, mode—what are students finding

_____ Highlight data column; use autosum to average. Notice the formula in the cell: =AVERAGE(H8:H15)

_____ Copy the formula and replace *AVERAGE* with Mean, median, or mode for that calc

Save to network; save-as to flash drive; close down (Alt+F4)

Excel is a favorite with students from 3ʳᵈ grade on when they discover formulas can add and subtract for them. Here are the skills I teach if I have time 1) after each speed quiz, 2) when I have extra time (for some reason—maybe students got a lesson much faster than I expected):

	A	B	C	D	E	F	G
1	**T2 SPEED QUIZ**						
2		WPM	Grade		**Teach this with each speed quiz:**		
3	1	22	9		*rename tab*		*font size*
4	2	21	10		*recolor tab*		*fill*
5	3	19	6		*enter data*		*merge cells*
6	4	14	8		*average column*		
7	5	21	8		**Teach this with 3-week training**		
8	6	24	8		*add count, min, max, median, mode*		
9	7	29	10		*add label for WPM and Grade*		
10	8	28	10		*add labels for formulas*		
11	9	19	9		*click on cells and see the formula*		
12	10	21	10		*add separater line under data*		
13	11	15	8		*B/I rows 21-24*		
14	12	17	10		*F11 graph*		
15	13	16	10			*Who's the slowest*	
16	14	19	10			*Who's the fastest*	
17	15	20	10			*Who got the highest grade*	
18	16	18	10			*Who got the lowest grade*	
19	17	14	10		*Format Graph*		
20	18	20	10			*rt click--chart options*	
21	average	19.83333	9.222222			*explore chart options*	
22	median	19.5	10			*rt-click--chart type*	
23	mode	21	10			*change colors*	
24	count	18	18			*change background*	
25	max	29	10				
26	min	14	6				
27							

Lesson #8—Halloween Story

Vocabulary	Problem solving	Collaborations
☐ Clip-art ☐ Font ☐ Cursor ☐ Grammar check ☐ Log-on ☐ Red 'X' ☐ Print preview	☐ How do I spell-check (F7) ☐ What if program disappears (look on taskbar)? ☐ I deleted my story (push Ctrl+Z) ☐ My screen is too small (click + in lower right corner)	☐ Spelling ☐ Grammar ☐ Composition

NETS-S Standards
1. Creativity and innovation; 2. Communication; 6. Technology operations

Lesson questions? Go to http://askatechteacher.com

Problem solving Board—continue presentations
Homework—don't forget to turn it in the last day of the month

Lesson plan: Students write a brief story in MS Word paying attention to proper story-writing technique, grammar and spelling. Use this project to review all the MS Word skills students have honed since 2nd grade. When those are done, have students add a few advanced skills—like watermarks.

_____ Open Word; review layout. Type story using correct writing techniques learned in class. Use a story written in the classroom or one they make up during tech time. Remind them it's only a few paragraphs—one to introduce, one to share the plot's drama, and one to close. See sample on next page.

_____ Use WordArt for title; center with alignment tools

_____ Click inside five words to change font, font size and font color

_____ Insert 5 clipart pictures to go along with story. Remember: image goes where cursor is blinking

_____ Insert a festive holiday page border. Use dialogue box to change color and thickness as desired

_____ Insert watermark, either 'Happy Halloween' text or picture

_____ Spell check and grammar check; explain that grammar-check is often wrong so students must decide themselves whether to accept corrections; print preview— does the story fit on one page? Resize pictures if necessary

_____ Have students review work with grading rubric (see next pages)

_____ Save to network folder with Ctrl+S. Print (Ctrl+P)

Close down to desktop (Alt+F4)

"Error, no keyboard – press **F1** to continue."

TRICK TREAT

Halloween

5th Grade Technology |**Page 40**

HALLOWEEN STORY

Your name
Your teacher
Date

HALLOWEEN STORY

A man was walking home alone late one night when he hears......

...BUMP... BUMP... BUMP...

...behind him. He looks back, and sees a coffin banging towards him.

BUMP... BUMP... BUMP...

Terrified, the man runs home, coffin bouncing behind him ...

... faster... BUMP... BUMP... BUMP.

He fumbles with his keys, rushes in, and locks the door.
The coffin crashes through his door, lid clapping ...

clappity BUMP... CLAPPITY-BUMP... clappity-BUMP

His heart's pounding; head reeling; breath coming in sobbing

gasps. With a loud CRASH the coffin

comes bumping and clapping towards him. Desperate, he
throws a basket of Halloween candy at the apparition.
Now what happens???

Happy Halloween

HALLOWEEN GRADING RUBRIC

1. Heading with name, date, teacher   _____
2. Several paragraphs of story   _____
   a. 5 different fonts   _____
   b. 5 different size fonts   _____
   c. 5 different colors   _____
   d. Spell-check   _____
   e. Grammar check   _____
3. A festive border   _____
4. A WordArt title   _____
5. 5 pictures—all the same size   _____
6. *One text box with a quote (extra)*   _____
7. *Watermark*   _____
8. *Call-out attached to a picture*   _____
9. *Autoshape with fill color*   _____
10. Story fills page, but not more   _____
11. Check Print Preview—only one page _____
12. Professional appearance   _____

Italics are for extra credit—they are extensions on learning

Q: Where do baby ghosts go during the day?

A: Day scare centers
http://www.kidsdomain.com/holiday/halloween/games/jokes.html

Lesson #9—Searching the Internet

Vocabulary	Problem solving	Collaborations
☐ Search bar ☐ Address bar ☐ Quotes ☐ Refine search ☐ Limiters ☐ Hits ☐ Extension ☐ Domain	☐ I deleted my work (Ctrl+Z) ☐ What's today's date (Shift+Alt+D) ☐ My browser toolbar disappeared (push F11) ☐ My browser is too small (double click title bar) ☐ My browser text is too small (Push Ctrl+ to zoom in)	☐ Grammar ☐ Spelling ☐ Social studies ☐ Geography
NETS-S Standards		
3. Research and information Fluency; 4. Problem solving and decision making		

Lesson questions? Go to http://askatechteacher.com

Problem solving Board—continue presentations
Type to Learn or online keyboarding program; Good posture, hand position

_____ Don't forget homework—due monthly

Lesson plan: Show students how to use Google search tools to research and find specific files. Use Google to convert money, see what time it is around the world, add numbers, define a word and more. Students have a lot of fun trying the different tools.

_____ Open Google.com; discuss difference between a search bar and an address bar

_____ Type 'solar system' (no quotes) into the search bar or use a term students are studying in the classroom.

_____ Now type "solar system" (with quotes)—the quotes refine hits. How many websites come up now?

_____ Next, type "solar system" mars—adding a word refines hits more

_____ Now type "solar system" –mars. This leaves out sites about Mars

_____ Look at the hits that come up. Notice the extensions—.org, .edu, .net, .com. Discuss the differences, what these extensions mean and how they can be used to find the websites most suited to a student's search

_____ Try other search skills listed on the next pages. Find definitions, find names in the phonebook, use calculator functions, convert currencies, find area codes and specific file types, find specific site types and similar sites, find the time around the world and use * as a general term

Close down to desk top

HOW TO SEARCH ON GOOGLE

Definitions	Define: computer definitions of the word computer from Web.
Phonebook	Phonebook: Murray Irvine Phonebook for people named 'murray' in Irvine
Calculator	33 + 33 provides the answer to any function
Converter	Converts currencies. I.e. 45 US dollars in yen
Area Code Finder	'949' shows geographic location with this area code
File type finder	'civil war filetype:ppt finds PowerPoints on Civil War
Site type finder	'site:.edu lincoln' finds .edu websites about Lincoln 'site:UK Iraq' finds British websites about Iraq
Similar sites	type 'related:' followed by the website address: 'related:www.google.com'
License plate finder	Type plate number into search bar
Time finder	'time in New York' tells you current time in New York
Fill in the blank	Use asterisk in sentence and Google will fill it in with the correct information. I.e. 'Mt. Everest is * feet high.

"A printer consists of three main parts: the case, the jammed paper tray and the blinking red light"

HOW TO SEARCH ON GOOGLE

If you type...	You will find pages containing...
Hawaii Vacation	Webpages with the words **Hawaii** and **vacation**
Maui OR Hawaii	Webpages with the word **Maui** or **Hawaii**
"To each his own"	Webpages with the exact phrase "**to each his own**"
Virus –computer	Webpages with the word **virus** but NOT **computer**
"Star Trek" fan	Webpages with the phrase "**Star Trek**" and fan
To find info, type it as a sentence with an asterisk for the unknown.	

HOW TO SEARCH ON GOOGLE

HOW TO SEARCH ON GOOGLE

Definitions	Define:word; internet definitions of a word, i.e., define:computer from Web.
Phonebook	Phonebook:Harris Irvine; a white pages for people named "Harris' in Irvine
Calculator	33 + 33 provides answer to any function (+, -, *, /)
Converter	Converts currencies. I.e., '45 US dollars in yen'
Area Code Finder	'949' shows geographic location with this area code
File type finder	filetype:ppt "Civil War" finds PowerPoints on Civil War
Site type finder	Site:edu lincoln finds .edu websites about Lincoln
Similar sites	related:website.com finds websites similar to the one entered; i.e.,; 'related:www.google.com'
License plate finder	Type plate number into search bar
Time finder	'time in New York' tells you current time in New York
Fill in the blank	Use asterisk in sentence and Google will fill it with the correct information. I.e., 'Mt. Everest is * feet high.

/ord

Collaborations
☐ *Grammar*
☐ *Spelling*
☐ *Research*
☐ *Science*

gy operations

acher.com

ure and hands

n table in MS Word. They
ean, find an example and
e with classroom research
to make Word tables.

t page). What's the http,
eek's discussion on what
ho can get them. Explain
material on the site.
e surfing (see websites in

her)
mportance', 'extensions',

extensions, starting at
ut column together and

ortance relative to other

f the webpage using <u>Jing</u>
Paste and crop if needed
te in cell by its extension
enter or adding a space
this address.
for back-up. Check print
then print
te; students can do this
ting in second grade)
down to desktop
for ideas) on the class

ELEMENTS OF WEB ADDRESS

You enter the URL of a site by typing it into the **Address** bar of your web browser, just under the toolbar.

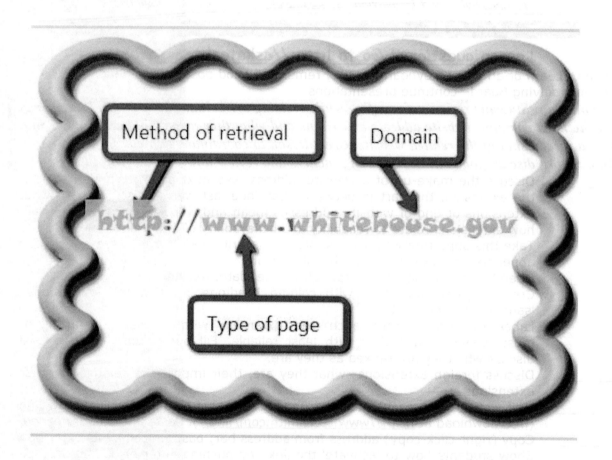

WEBSITE ADDRESSES

Name

Date

Teacher

Importance	Extension	Sample	Screen Print
1	.org	http://www.seds.org/nineplanets/nineplanets/overview.html	
2	.gov	http://solarsystem.nasa.gov/kids/index.cfm	
3	.edu	http://tes.asu.edu/	
4	.net	http://www.astrobio.net/news/index.php	
5	.com	http://www.enchantedlearning.com/subjects/astronomy/solarsystem/	
6	.foreign	http://www.bbc.co.uk/science/space/solarsystem/mars/index.shtml	

Using an Internet Start Page

An internet start page is the first page that comes up when students select the internet icon. It should include everything students visit on a daily basis (typing websites, research locations, sponge sites) as well as information specific to the current project, class  guidelines, the day's 'to do' list, and a calculator. It is one of the great ways teachers can make internetting simpler and safer for their students.

Mine includes oft-used websites, blog sites, a To Do list, search tools, email, a calendar of events, pictures of interest, rss feeds of interest, weather, news, a graffiti wall and more. Yours will be different. I used protopage.com, but you can use netvibes or pageflakes.com. Each comes with its own collection of installable 'widgets' to personalize the page to your needs.

Start pages are an outreach of the ever-more-popular social networking. Most search engines offer them also (try iGoogle at www.google.com/ig). They all have a huge library of custom fields (called 'flakes' on Pageflakes) to  individualize any home page. And, they're all simple. Don't be intimidated.

When you get yours set up, on the To Do list, put what the child should do to start each computer time. This gives them a sense of independence, adultness, as they get started while you're wrapping something else up.

Lesson #11—Holiday Flier

Vocabulary	Problem solving	Collaborations
☐ Icon ☐ Right-click ☐ Ctrl+S ☐ Crop ☐ Handles	☐ I can't find the Picture Tools ribbon (check the top center) ☐ How do I print (Ctrl+P) ☐ How do I save (Ctrl+S) ☐ How do I paste (Ctrl+V)	☐ Spelling ☐ Grammar ☐ Art—graphics
NETS-S Standards 4. Problem solving; 6. Technology operations and concepts		

Lesson questions? Go to http://askatechteacher.com

Problem solving Board—continue presentations

Type to Learn or online keyboard site—good posture and hand position

_____ Remember keyboarding homework due at end of month

Lesson plan: Create a holiday flier using Publisher template. Choose a one-page template and adapt text, picture, colors, layout, etc. This project is very easy so I use it to remind students how fun and simple computers are and how much they've learned since they began in kindergarten.

_____ Open Publisher; go to Quick Publications

_____ Select a template ; adjust color and font schemes on the right sidebar to the current holiday; click 'create'

_____ Delete current picture and replace with one that fits the holiday (insert-clipart); resize using corner handles so it fills space available

_____ Advanced: Go to Google images; search for and select a holiday image; go to full-size image; right-click copy and then right-click paste onto the Publisher holiday flier (see sample on next pages)

_____ Advanced: Use crop tool (find it on picture ribbon) to select just the part of the picture that is required (i.e., the car and not the luggage)

_____ Advanced: Use the 'Picture tools' ribbon to add borders and shadows to the image

_____ Change Heading and Subheading to create holiday greeting with student name

_____ Save with Ctrl+S; print with Ctrl+P

Close down to desk top; save to network file folder

Lesson #12—Newsletter in Publisher

Vocabulary	Problem solving	Collaborations
☐ *Ctrl* ☐ *Text box* ☐ *Placeholder* ☐ *Dialogue box*	☐ *What time is it? (Shift+Alt+D)* ☐ *My typing disappeared (Ctrl+Z)* ☐ *How do I undo? (Ctrl+Z)* ☐ *My screen froze (clear a dialogue box)*	☐ *Art* ☐ *Vocabulary* ☐ *Grammar* ☐ *Spelling*

NETS-S Standards
1. Creativity; 2. Communication and collaboration

Lesson questions? Go to http://askatechteacher.com

Problem solving Board—Finish presentations

Type to Learn—good posture; correct hand position

Sign up for Google Earth Board Presentations (info on next pages); start next week

_____ Students select a date to present and a location from 1) list of places they visited during fourth grade, 2) Wonders of the World, or 3) ???. I've included the list my classes used last year for examples.

_____ Use research skills to find one Fascinating Fact about the location to share with classmates. Allow students to skip a 45-minute homework to give them 45 minutes to do their research.

_____ Fill out information on study guide (see next pages) including Fascinating Fact.

_____ Grading will be based on criteria listed on rubric (see next pages)

Lesson plan: Students collaborate on a holiday newsletter or a class unit (colonies, animals, etc.). Pick a template. Add text and pictures. See sample on next pages.

_____ Have two stories completed prior to coming to tech class.

_____ Select 'Newsletters' template; change font/color schemes (on rt) if desired

_____ Name newsletter; add a slogan (in place of 'Business name')

_____ Copy-paste stories about holidays at school and at home from Word docs previously prepared; add a title to each article; add one picture per story

_____ Use drop cap to start each article; add one picture per story to make it more visual; complete 'Inside this Issue' with article headings

_____ Use sidebar box ('Special Points of Interest) to highlight foods, activities, or anything special for the holidays

_____ Print; save to network file folder; save-as to flash drive as back-up

Close down to desktop (Alt+F4)

Keyboard Emoticons			
O:)	Angel	:*	Kiss
:D	Big Grin	:-#	Lips are sealed
:]	Blockhead	:-{	Mustache
:-C	Bummer	@}-;-'—	Rose
=^..^=	Cat	:<	Sad
:'(	Crying	:-\	Undecided
:-)'	Drooling	;)	Wink
}:>	Evil	:-*	Yuck

GOOGLE EARTH BOARD SIGN-UP

Pick a date and a location—so sign your name twice

	Class A	B	C
Week of Dec. 15th			
Week of Jan. 5th			
Week of Jan. 12th			
Week of Jan. 19th			
Week of Jan 26th			
Week of Feb. 2nd			
Week of Feb. 9th			
Week of Feb. 23rd			
Week of Mar. 2nd			

Pick a Location:	Class A	B	C
Egyptian Pyramids			
Great Wall of China			
Stonehenge			
Hagia Sophia, Istanbul			
Leaning Tower of Pisa			
The Eiffel Tower			
Panama Canal			
Taj Mahal			
Victoria Falls			
Ngorongoro Crater			
Mt. Everest			
Ayers Rock			
The Ross Ice Shelf			
Tierra del Fuego			
Straits of Gibraltar			
The Red Sea			
Mt. St. Helens			
San Andreas Fault			
Great African Rift			
Madagascar			
Istanbul			
Siberia			
Death Valley			
Suez Canal			
Vatican City			
The Chunnel			

GOOGLE EARTH BOARD PROJECT

Your name:_____

Your Teacher_____

Estimated time: 45 minutes

1. Write your Google Earth Board location here:_____
2. Write the date of your class presentation here:_____
3. Find your location on Google Earth
4. Print a picture of your location from Google Earth and paste it here:

5. Look up one interesting fact about this location and write it here:

_____

_____

_____

_____

6. When you make your presentation, turn this sheet in to me, filled out
7. Grading will be based on:
    a. Were you prepared on the correct date:
    b. Did you have a picture:
    c. Did you have an interesting fact:
    d. Did you speak loud enough for seat 19 to hear:
    e. Did you avoid 'umms', etc
    f. Did you look the audience in the eye as you talked:
8. You may skip a homework. Put the number of the one you are skipping here:_____

Notes:

- Type the location name in as it is written on the Google Earth Board. That is your best chance of finding it

- Turn off the markers for community notations (the check box that comes up under the 'fly to' locations) before saving the picture

- Save picture as 'file—save—save image' and then select your flash drive

- Turn your 3D buildings on (under 'layers')

- Be sure to pan in so we can clearly see your location or building

- You can get the interesting fact from the encyclopedia, Wikipedia, your parents, or something you learned in class

- If you can't find a location, try the Google Earth Community for a link (for example, use the Community for Ross Ice Shelf)

- If you know the location, you may go there without using the 'fly to' option; just add your own place marker (this might work better for 'San Andreas Fault' and the 'Great African Rift')

GOOGLE EARTH BOARD GRADING

Name: _____

Class: _____

You were prepared with filled-out project sheet   _____

Your project sheet had a picture of your location   _____

You shared an interested fact with the class   _____

You spoke loudly enough for all to hear   _____

You seemed knowledgeable   _____

You had a calm, confident presence   _____

You didn't use vocal cues that showed nervousness   _____

You didn't use visual cues that showed nervousness   _____

You looked your audience in the eye as you talked   _____

Overall impression   _____

PUBLISHER NEWSLETTER

Lesson #13—Holiday Calendar

Vocabulary	Problem solving	Collaborations
☐ Template	☐ I can't exit program (Alt+F4)	☐ Spelling
☐ Publisher	☐ I lost my doc (save early, save	☐ Grammar
☐ wpm	often)	☐ Science
☐ Home row	☐ Screen froze (clear dialogue box)	☐ Presentation skills
☐ Geek	☐ Document disappeared (check	☐ Problem-solving skills
☐ Template	taskbar)	

NETS-S Standards

1. Creativity and innovation; 2. Communication and collaboration

Lesson questions? Go to http://askatechteacher.com

Keyboard—Remember: keyboard speed goal is 30 wpm by the end of the year

_____ Good posture; correct hand position; keep eyes on screen, elbows at sides
Google Earth Board presentations start today.

_____ Students present their research and take audience questions

_____ Grade based on knowledge, confidence, and presentation.

Lesson plan: Create a calendar of student holiday activities. Students can pick their template, add text and pictures. Pictures can be copy-pasted from an internet search. Students can work in groups or singly.

_____ Open Publisher; select a calendar template; set calendar date for one month (on right sidebar). Change color schemes and font schemes to holiday preference

_____ Change pictures to match the holiday theme

_____ Go over upcoming events together. Have students share what they're doing, concerts and vacations, and add each to the calendar in the correct date. Resize font as needed to fit in the calendar cell. Add only one event per date. If there's a conflict between a school event and a personal one, have student select.

_____ Advanced: Add a picture to date cell to enhance event (see example). Resize to small so it fits nicely in the calendar date cell
Add student name to the lower right cell.

_____ Print (Ctrl+P); save (Ctrl+S) to network; save-as to flash drive as back-up
Internet—for those finished—visit www.pbs.org/wgbh/nova/programs.html

If you were a computer

* You could add/remove someone in your life using the control panel
* You could put your kids (or parents) in the recycle bin and restore them when you feel like it
* You could improve your appearance by adjusting the display settings
* You could turn off the speakers when life gets too noisy

DECEMBER 2011

PUBLISHER CALENDAR

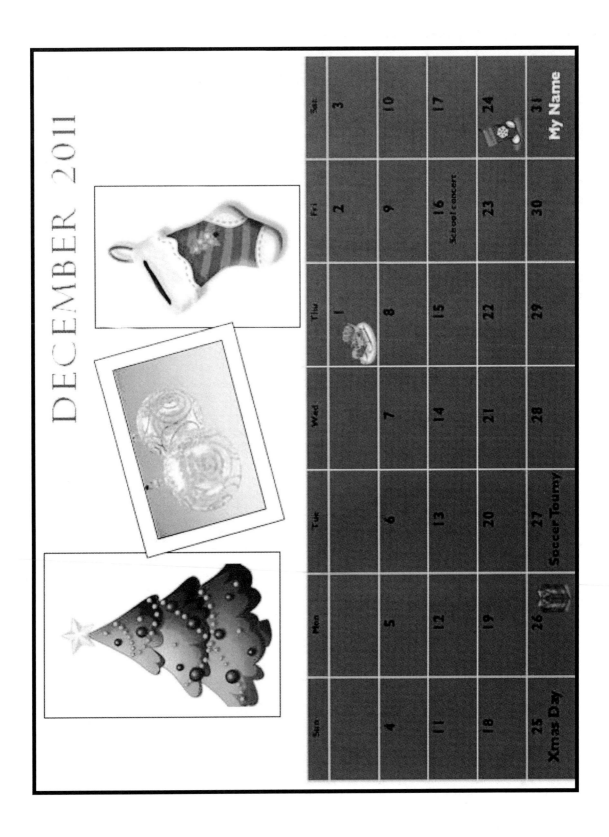

DECEMBER 2011

Sun	Mon	Tue	Wed	Thu	Fri	Sat
				1	2	3
4	5	6	7	8	9	10
11	12	13	14	15	16 School concert	17
18	19	20	21	22	23	24
25 Xmas Day	26	27 Soccer Tourny	28	29	30	31 My Name

Lesson #14—Trifold in Publisher I

Vocabulary	Problem solving	Collaborations
☐ Drill down ☐ Graphic ☐ Network	☐ Screen froze (Is dialogue box open?) ☐ Can't exit program (Alt+F4)	☐ History ☐ Graphic Art ☐ Grammar/Spelling

NETS-S Standards
3. Research and information fluency; 5. Digital citizenship

Lesson questions? Go to http://askatechteacher.com

Type to Learn or <u>Dance Mat Typing</u>—good posture; curved hands; home row

_____   Speed quiz next week. Goal: 30 wpm

Google Earth Board presentations continue

Lesson plan: Three week project to create a Publisher trifold brochure to support a unit of inquiry in the classroom. Students add lots of detail and lots of research on different aspects of colonization.

_____   Review Publisher layout —text boxes, design elements, etc. Explain the purpose of a trifold—panels, text and pictures on each section, title panel, back panel and inside 3-inside three-panel display as the meat of the brochure. See project sample on next pages. Print it, fold it as a trifold so students can see the power of this sort of brochure presentation.

_____   Open Publisher. Select 'Brochures'. Select one you like. Adjust font and color schemes on right sidebar to suit your taste and push 'create'.

_____   Start with Page 1, Panel 3: Delete all text boxes. Add WordArt title for your colony; add picture of colony; add text box at bottom with your name, teacher, date (see inset below)

_____   Page 1, Panel 2 (back of trifold): Add a map of your colony or an overview; add text box with title, 'Why colonists emigrated to this colony'. Fill in a discussion about that topic (see inset below).

_____   Page 1, Panel 1: Enter text box with the first of 4 questions you'll answer about colonization. Keep all titles bold, centered, font 16. Type answer. Fill in remaining white space with design elements from Design Gallery (boxes, checkerboards, etc.) and/or picture

_____   Save to your file folder (ctrl+S); save-as to flash drive as back-up. What's the difference between 'save' and 'save-as'?

Why did the settlers leave their home?

- To find a better life
- For religious freedom
- To be able to have their own religious beliefs
- To get better land and go to their own church
- Have a free-run government.

Moving to Massachusetts will get you great land, a free government, and amazing churches and people. We have gotten to know many Indians, who happen to be nice, and they have taught us how to make, harvest, and eat corn. If you're looking for exotic and different foods, come to Massachusetts!

Massachusetts Colony

Student
Teacher

How did natives react to the settlers?

The natives, at first, wanted to keep their distance, but at the same time, were mad at them for stealing their

land and curious, too. Eventually, they got a chance to meet the settlers, and began to take their chance to teach them how to harvest and make corn. After that, the settlers and the natives began to become friends, and enjoyed their first Thanksgiving!!

Was colonization a success or failure?

The colonization was a definite success. The settlers learned how to plant, grow, harvest, and eat many crops, and became friends with the so-called mean natives. Most Survived the first winter, and as know, they created a village, learned to eat, met a native, and had Thanksgiving! Their colonization was a complete success!!

Did they create a government?

Yes, they created a government and it was a type of democracy, but only men who belonged to the church could join.

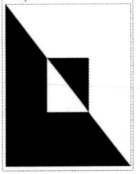

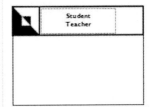

Student
Teacher

Lesson #15—Trifold in Publisher II

Vocabulary	Problem solving	Collaborations
☐ wpm ☐ Design gallery ☐ Dolch ☐ Copy-paste ☐ Tri-fold ☐ Brochure ☐ Handles	☐ My monitor doesn't work (wake up mouse, check power) ☐ My computer doesn't work (check power, check plug) ☐ My volume doesn't work (check volume control, check headphones connection)	☐ Spelling ☐ Grammar ☐ Humanities—history ☐ Vocabulary

NETS-S Standards
3. Research and information fluency; 5. Digital citizenship

Lesson questions? Go to http://askatechteacher.com

Keyboarding—Type to Learn or an online keyboard site as warm-up. See hints on next pages

Speed quiz—Grade is based on improvement from first quiz (20%=10/10; 10-19%=9/10; 1-9%=8/10; 0%=7/10; slower=6/10). Remind students they are not competing against the best typists in the class, only against themselves

_____ Open Word; type in heading—name, date, teacher

_____ Type for 5 minutes using a typing sample (see below); spell-check for 1 minute

_____ Find word count (lower left corner) and type at bottom of page

_____ Save (Ctrl+S); save-as to flash drive; print (Ctrl+P)

Google Earth Board presentations—continue

Publisher—tri-fold brochure project

_____ Page 2: Put one question as heading on each of the three panels. Headings are font 16, bold, centered. Answer questions students have been assigned

_____ Take a moment to check all headings. Do they match? Size, font, color should.

_____ Type in answers to all questions. Use good grammar, spelling. Double space (rather than indent) between paragraphs. Make sure text formatting matches—size 14, TNR (or whichever font was selected), spacing set at 1.15 or 1.5 for all entries

_____ Save (Ctrl+S); Print(Ctrl+P)

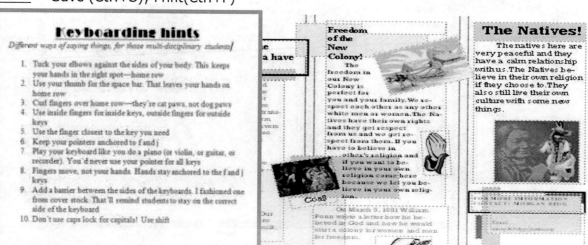

Another Sample Keyboard Speed Quiz

The Best Thing In The World

Once upon a time, four princes lived in a faraway land. Their father was old. One day he said he would not live long now. His sons must start out into the world. In a year, bring back the best thing they found. The one who could pick the best thing would be the new king.

The first brother said he would look in every city or town to buy the best thing for his father. The next two brothers said they would both go on fast ships over the sea to find something better.

The last brother said he was going to ask the people here in their own land to tell him the best thing. The other three began to laugh and told him he would never be king. The last brother started off. When he had gone about six miles, he met a man. He asked him what he was carrying in his big bags. The man told him it was the best thing in the world. They were full of good nuts which fell from his five trees.

The brother didn't think that would work and decided to himself he must try again.

He went another seven miles and found a small brown bird. It had been hurt, so he put it in his coat where it could keep warm. As he went on, he saw a little girl crying. He ran to meet her and asked why she was crying? She said she wanted to get some water from the well. She and her family used so much. They drank cold water. They washed their clothes clean with hot water. But she didn't know how to pull it up and asked the prince to show her.

The brother asked her to hold his bird and said he would help her. He told her it didn't fly around anymore because it got its wing hurt.

**This passage contains many of the 220 Dolch Basic Sight Words.
Adapted from
http://www.bristolvaschools.org/mwarren/DolchWords.htm**

KEYBOARDING HINTS

These came directly from the classroom, tested on 400 students a year. These are the most common fixes that help students excel at keyboarding:

1. Tuck elbows against the sides of your body. This keeps hands in the right spot—home row

2. Use your RIGHT thumb for the space bar. That leaves hands on home row

3. Curl fingers over home row—they're cat paws, not dog paws

4. Use inside fingers for inside keys, outside fingers for outside keys

5. Use the finger closest to the key you need. Sounds simple, but this isn't what usually happens with beginners.

6. Keep pointers anchored to *f* and *j*

7. Play keyboard like a piano (or violin, or guitar, or recorder). You'd never use your pointer for all keys

8. Fingers move, not your hands. Hands stay anchored to the *f* and *j* keys

9. Don't use caps lock for capitals! Use shift.

10. Add a barrier between sides of the keyboards. I fashioned one from cover stock. That'll remind students to stay on the correct side of keyboard

Lesson #16—Trifold in Publisher III

Vocabulary	Problem solving	Collaborations
☐ Design gallery ☐ Text box ☐ Desk top publishing ☐ Drill down ☐ Trifold ☐ Rubric ☐ Network	☐ How do I close a program (Alt+F4) ☐ My program disappeared (check taskbar) ☐ My typing disappeared (Ctrl+Z)	☐ Spelling ☐ Grammar ☐ Humanities—history

NETS-S Standards:
3. Research and information fluency; 5. Digital citizenship

Lesson questions? Go to http://askatechteacher.com

Type to Learn or online keyboarding websites—remember monthly homework

_____ Good posture; Correct hand position, curved over home row

Google Earth Board—continue presentations

Extra: Vocabulary assessment—ungraded. Include all words collected during last year's fifth grade and current Speak Like a Geek presentations.

_____ When done, practice Type to Learn or website that collaborates with classroom discussions. Include 3-4 on the class internet start page (www.protopage.com/smaatech#Untitled/Fifth_Grade)

Open Publisher tri-fold project—final week working on this

_____ Typing finished last week. Check trifold for grammar and spelling. Review to be sure all sentences make sense

_____ If there's blank white space, go to Design Gallery; insert design elements that fit the topic and fill remaining space. Design elements include: accessory bar, accent boxes, marquis

_____ Review rubric (see next pages) to be sure all required pieces are included.

_____ Print both pages; fold as a trifold with white sides back-to-back; staple in corners to keep pages together

_____ Save to network; save-as to flash drive. Print (Ctrl+P).

Close down to desk top (Alt+F4)

SAMPLE FIFTH GRADE VOCABULARY QUIZ

Name:_____

Teacher:_____

Select a word from the word bank and write it under the definition it matches. It must be spelled correctly for full credit.

Cell	Refine	Template	.gov
Extension	search	.com	.org
Hits	Scheme	.edu	

1. A website extension that identifies the site as a commercial site
   _____

2. A layout used to create documents
   _____

3. A website extension that identifies the site as non-profit, non-government
   _____

4. One of the boxes in a table or an Excel spreadsheet
   _____

5. An orderly combination of colors, fonts that deliver a professional appearance to a desktop publishing document
   _____

6. A website extension that identifies the site as a government agency
   _____

7. The three letter extension that tells a user a document was saved in Word
   _____

8. A website extension that identifies an educational institution, usually a university
   _____

9. Enter additional term(s) to narrow a search, such as "" and +
   _____

10. The number of matches made by a search engine like Google in a search
   _____

Use this template and replace with words of your choice from Appendix or Ask a Tech Teacher website

PUBLISHER TRIFOLD BROCHURE
Grading Rubric

Your name: _____

Your homeroom teacher: _____

---

1. Title Page **4 points** _____
   a. *Eye catching and clear* _____
   b. *All fonts match* _____
   c. *Brochure title stands out* _____
   d. *Your name and class in smaller font* _____
   e. *White space filled* _____
   f. *Grammar and spelling* _____

2. Back page **4 points** _____
   a. *Eye catching and clear* _____
   b. *All fonts match* _____
   c. *Picture and text fill white space* _____
   d. *Grammar and spelling* _____

3. Inside **9 points** _____
   a. *Headings in larger font* _____
   b. *All fonts match* _____
   c. *No white spaces* _____
   d. *Pictures fit events discussed* _____
   e. *Spell-check* _____
   f. *Grammar check* _____

4. Overall Professional Look **3 points** _____
   (inside print lines, attractive look, organized, easy to understand, etc.)

How I grade myself: _____
   Explain: _____
   _____

Lesson #17—Word: Basically Advanced I

Vocabulary	Problem solving	Collaborations
☐ Macro ☐ Default ☐ Text box ☐ Option ☐ Lab ☐ Assessment	☐ How do I capitalize (use shift key or caps lock for all letters) ☐ My capital won't go off (is caps lock on?) ☐ What's my user name? ☐ What's my password? ☐ What's the date (Shift+Alt+D)	☐ Spelling ☐ Grammar
NETS-S Standards: 2. Communication; 4. Critical thinking			

Lesson questions? Go to http://askatechteacher.com

Type to Learn or online keyboard site. Watch posture and hand position
Google Earth Board—continue presentations

It's a good idea to constantly cycle back on skills students have learned so they don't forget them, especially those that they will be expected to know throughout school. In this project, students are asked to complete a list of tasks in Word to determine their knowledge. Give it midway through the year. Depending upon the results, you may want to adjust future projects to include more or less MS Word training.

_____ Open MS Word; Use macro to add heading (review macro)

_____ Have students follow all directions on the next sheet. Do not answer questions for them. If they are stuck, they should move on to the next skill. All skills have been covered between 2nd and 5th grade. Adjust the assessment as needed to satisfy particular circumstances. You may choose to make this a collaborative exercise (where they work in groups) or individual.

_____ See sample of assessment on next page. This will take at least thirty minutes. It may take longer. Adjust requirements and grading as needed.

_____ Have students verify that a document will print in the school lab by checking to see which is the default printer in the tech room.

_____ Use the rubric (see next pages) to grade accomplished skills for the class. It will let you see where there are holes in the class's learning.

_____ Save to file folder and Print

Those who are finished: provide a list of sponge activities on the class internet start page (see suggestions on next pages).

> "I have traveled the length and breadth of this country and talked with the best people, and I can assure you that data processing is a fad that won't last out the year."
> – The editor in charge of business books for Prentice Hall, 1957

WORD ASSESSMENT

Follow the instructions below. Part of the assessment is how well you read and complete directions. Do your best. If you don't remember how to do a skill, go on to the next.

- Put your heading on page
- Right-align heading
- Put a title underneath heading——"Word Assessment"
- Center the title, font Comic Sans, font size 14, bold
  - Type two paragraphs about yourself, font size 12, Times New Roman
- Change the second paragraph to font size 16 and Papyrus
- Add bullets with
  1. Your daily activities
  2. What you like to read
  3. Who you play with
- Add "The End" as WordArt at the bottom of the page
- Add a border

> *Wherever you are, be there until you leave.*
> *—Anonymous*

- Add a picture
- Have text wrap around the clipart
- Put a call-out aimed at the picture
- Add an autoshape
- Color the autoshape pink or red
- Insert a footer

- Add a text box with what your mom said the most this summer
- Shade the text box
- Add a table with seven columns and three times during the day
- Add information for each day and each time of day

Sunday	Monday	Tuesday	Wednesday	Thursday	Friday	Saturday
Ate breakfast						
Ate lunch						
Ate dinner						

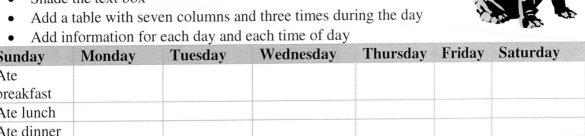

Grading Sheet for Word Assessment

WORD ASSESSMENT

Question	STUDENT																		
	1	2	3	4	5	6	7	8	9	10	11	12	13	14	15	16	17	18	19
1 heading																			
all parts																			
2 right align																			
3 title																			
underneath																			
4 center																			
Comic sans																			
size 14																			
bold																			
5 2 paragraphs																			
size 12																			
TNR																			
6 Para. 2																			
size 16																			
Papyrus																			
7 bullets																			
daily activities																			
ate																			
played w/																			
8 The End																			
Wordart																			
page bottom																			
9 border																			
10 picture																			
11 text wrap																			
12 call-out																			
location																			
13 autoshape																			
14 pink																			
15 footer																			
16 text box																			
mom's words																			
17 shade text box																			
18 table																			
7 columns																			
3 rows																			
heading row																			
19 table into																			
Total	0	0	0	0	0	0	0	0	0	0	0	0	0	0	0	0	0	0	0

Thirty-two Ways to Use Spare Classroom Time

I keep a list of themed websites that are easy-in easy-out for students. They must be activities that can be accomplished enjoyably in less than ten minutes. In the parlance, these are called "sponges".

You may have read my post with nineteen sites my students love visiting during sponge time (let me know if you liked them, have some to add, I'm always interested in learning from you). Here are thirty-two more. Hope you like them!

Language Arts

- Make your own Story—answer questions, and the story writes itself
- Funny poetry to read and enjoy
- Jeff's Poetry for Kids
- Fill in the blank poetry
- Get Writing—write your own story
- Web version of Mad Libs

Math

- Math and Virtual Manipulatives
- Math website—popular, a standard
- Math—by Grade Level
- Math—game-oriented
- Mental Math
- Minute Math

Research

- All-around research site
- Research for kids
- School Tube—learning videos organized by topics
- World Book Online

- Research—chapters on subjects
- National Geographic for kids
- Nova video programs

Science

- Videos on science topics
- Visit a Virtual Farm
- Virtual weather, machines and surgery
- National Geographic Kids
- NOVA Videos—great topics Nova video programs
- Science Headlines—audio (grades 3+)
- Great site on yucky stuff
- Virtual tours

Technology

- Virtual tours
- Webcams around the World
- More Worldwide webcams for kids
- Nova video programs
- School Tube—learning videos from YouTube. Organized by topics

Photo credit: Cuangyuwando

Lesson #18—Excel Basics I

Vocabulary	Problem solving	Collaborations
☐ Row/Column ☐ Cell ☐ Excel ☐ Border ☐ Right-aligned	☐ I can't find my file folder (check log-in) ☐ My formula doesn't work (click the cell and check it)	☐ Math ☐ History ☐ Critical thinking skills ☐ Presentations

NETS-S Standards:
2.b; 4.c

Lesson questions? Go to http://askatechteacher.com

Type to Learn—or online typing website (see appendix for examples)

_____ Good posture; good hand position

Google Earth Board presentations—speak loudly and look audience in the eye

Excel basics—review of 3rd grade Excel: Show students how to use Excel formulas to add, subtract, multiply and divide. Have them practice with worksheets provided by the classroom teacher or the example on the next pages. Have them figure out the answers first and then check them against Excel's formulas.

_____ Open Excel; review worksheet parts (columns, rows, cells, menus, ribbons, bottom tabs). Explain how rows and columns define cells

_____ Double-click 'sheet one' tab; rename 'Auto Math'; push enter; right-click; select 'tab color' change tab color to one you like

_____ Go to A1—add title (Auto Math) with caps lock and font size 36; select cells A1-G1; merge-center (new skill for fifth graders); color with paint bucket

_____ Go to A2—add student name; go to A3—type 'Addition'; click on row 3—see how it selects the entire row; use paint bucket to color. Or, select A3-G3 and color with paint bucket (as shown in sample)

_____ Input all data (not answers). Use mental math to figure out the answers; jot them down on a sample sheet passed out by teacher

_____ Highlight bottom row of data; use border tool to add line (new 5th grade skill)

_____ Use Excel's formulas to solve each problem (start with = sign, use +, -, *, / for the function. The easiest way for students to create a formula is =; select first cell they want to use with a mouse click; input function—+,- /,*—then select the second cell they want to use; push enter for answer—see example on next page); complete the sheet

_____ Add the word 'Total' next to the answers in italics and right-align in cell

_____ Change the input numbers and see how Excel recalculates the answer!

_____ Go to print preview; switch to 'landscape'; adjust size; be sure everything is on one page; print

Close down to desk top (Alt+F4)

> "There is no reason anyone would want a computer in their home." -- Ken Olson, president, founder of Digital Equipment Corp., 1977

EXCEL SPREADSHEET

	A	B	C	D	E	F
1		AUTO MATH				
2	your name					
3	Addition					
4			26	144	720	1044	2583
5			13	12	20	2	3
6		Total	39				
7						
8	Subtraction					
9			26	144	720	1044	2583
10			13	12	20	2	3
11		Total	13				
12						
13	Multiplication					
14			26	144	720	1044	2583
15			13	12	20	2	3
16		Total	338				
17						
18	Division					
19			26	144	720	1044	2583
20			13	12	20	2	3
21		Total	2				

=C9-C10

1. type =
2. click first cell you want to use
3. type the function you want (+, -, * /)
4. Type second cell you want to use
5. Push enter

	29876	12
Total	5806	

Instructions:

double click 'sheet 2' tab and rename 'auto math'

rt click on 'auto math' tab and recolor

input title (caps lock, font size 36

input your name (rest of spreadsheet in font size 10)

input 'addition

click '3' and color row 3

input "total" and right-align

input data

add line under data

add using formula (equal sign, select first cell, +, select second cell, enter

change numbers to see how Excel adds for you

do subtraction, multiplication, division in same way

highlight from a1 to g1, merge-center, fill with paint bucket

print preview—set-up—change to landscape, change size to 175%

print page 1 only

Lesson #19—Excel Basics II

Vocabulary	Problem solving	Collaborations
☐ *Autosum* ☐ *Headings* ☐ *F11* ☐ *Axis* ☐ *Legend* ☐ *Worksheet*	☐ *I can't find my file folder (check log-in. Are you in correct root?)* ☐ *My screen froze (dialogue box open?)* ☐ *My graph is empty (make sure data is highlighted)* ☐ *Making a chart is confusing (try F1)*	☐ *Math* ☐ *Problem-solving*
NETS-S Standards: 2.b; 4.c		

Lesson questions? Go to http://askatechteacher.com

Type to Learn or online keyboarding websites (see appendix)

_____ Good posture; Correct hand position; use all fingers, keep eyes on screen
Google Earth Board presentations finish today. Anyone who hasn't, will present.

Lesson Plan: Collect data as a class. Input into Excel spreadsheet under assigned categories. Show students how to use F11 to create a chart and format the chart with ribbon tools and right-clicks.

_____ Have students open their Excel workbook (keep all Excel practice in same workbook by adding new tabs for new worksheets)

_____ Double-click 'sheet 3'; rename 'survey data'; recolor independently

_____ A1—add worksheet title (How I learn); A2—add student name; A3—add date (see example on next sheet)

_____ Project sample on next page onto SmartBoard or overhead so students can catch up or work ahead

_____ Add column headings (boys and girls) and choices (reading, writing, listening, talking, or create your own)

_____ Collect data as a class. Highlight data and push F11 to make chart;

_____ Right-click chart—format chart area; add title, labels to x and y axis, change background colors; resize title to 26; add your name after title; right-click chart background (this is the orange area in the chart below); format plot area. This is a review of 3rd, 4th grade, so students should work independently

_____ Change colors in legend—this is a new skill

Save to network; save-as to flash drive. What's the difference between 'save', 'save-as'? Print.

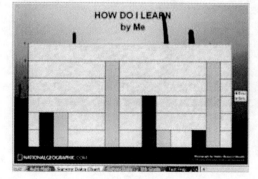

> *I cannot conceive that anybody will require multiplications at the rate of 40,000 or even 4,000 per hour …*
> — *F. H. Wales. 1936*

	A	B	C	D	E	F	G	H	I	J
1	HOW DO I LEARN									
2	your name						*Instructions:*			
3	1/13/2009					*double click 'sheet 3' tab and rename 'survey data'*				
4		Boys	Girls			*rt click on 'survey data' tab and recolor*				
5	Reading					*A1--input title (caps lock, font size 12)*				
6	Writing					*A2--input your name (rest of spreadheet in font size 10)*				
7	Listening					*A3--date (Ctrl+;)*				
8	Talking					*B3/B4, input 'boys', 'girls'*				
9						*A4-A8--input subjects*				
10						*survey class to collect data*				
11						*highlight from a1 to c1, merge-center; fill with paint bucket*				
12						*highlight from A4-c8; f11*				
13	WHEN I DO HOMEWORK									
14		Boys	Girls			*format chart*				
15	Do early					*add title, x and y labels*				
16	Do on time					*add backgrounds*				
17	Do late					*print preview--set-up--change to landscape, size to 175%*				
18	Don't do					*Print page 1 only*				

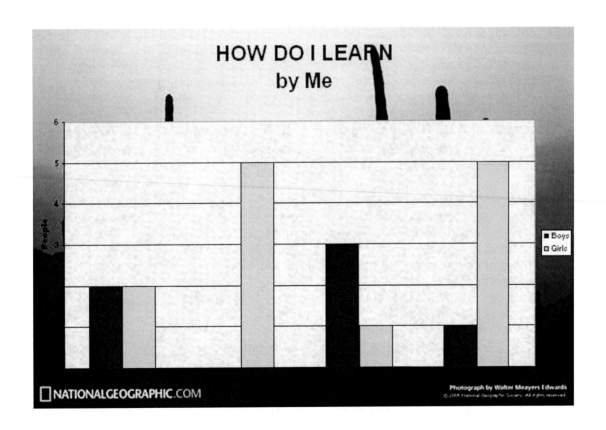

HOW DO I LEARN
by Me

Lesson #20—Excel Basics III

Vocabulary	Problem solving	Collaborations
☐ Tools ☐ Hyperlink ☐ Alphabetize ☐ Tabs ☐ Data ☐ Formula ☐ Function ☐ Geek ☐ Flash drive ☐ Format	☐ I can't exit (Alt+F4) ☐ I can't print (Ctrl+P) ☐ My document disappeared (use search; check taskbar) ☐ What's today's date (Ctrl+; in Excel—not like Shift+Alt+D in Word)	☐ Math ☐ Problem-solving
NETS-S Standards: 4. Problem solving; 5. Digital citizenship		

Lesson questions? Go to http://askatechteacher.com

Type to Learn—correct posture; Correct hand position
Sign up for Speak Like a Geek Vocabulary Board Presentations (see info on next pages); start next week

_____ As with problem solving board, students can get definition from family, friends, neighbors or teacher as a last resort. Students are responsible for teaching classmates what word means and using it in a sentence that shows they understand the meaning (i.e., *I like formatting* is not good; *I format my letter by adding borders and pictures* is good)

_____ Review grading (same as prior board—see next pages)

Lesson Plan: 22 of the simplest but most oft-used Excel skills (adding, alphabetizing, adding date, resizing, columns and rows, creating a chart, adding labels, adding images, adding hyperlink, etc.). Most is a review of 3rd and 4th grade Excel projects.

_____ Open current Excel workbook. Add a new worksheet named 'Basics'. Recolor.

_____ Do this together, as a class, then have students take it as a quiz (see next page). Remind students to put data in the correct cell. If they get stuck, move on to the next step; when finished, try Extra Credit

_____ Remember to push 'enter' to input data before formatting it

_____ Remember to start each formula with an = sign

_____ Remember: + = add, - = subtract, * = multiply, / = divide

_____ If there are skills that students didn't get to at this point in the year, replace them with others or skip

_____ There are two extra credit items to help students make up for problems they forgot how to solve. Use these, or add different ones more suited to your students.

_____ When finished, upload quiz to drop box or save to file folder and teacher will grade it from there. Be sure to save it correctly!

Save (Ctrl+S); save-as to flash drive; Close using Alt+F4

Speak Like a Geek

	Teacher #1	Teacher #2	Teacher #3
Week of Jan 24th			
Week of Jan. 31st			
Week of March 7th			
Week of March 14th			
Week of March 28th			
Week of April 11th			
Week of April 18th			
Week of April 25th			
Week of May 2nd			
	Teacher #1	Teacher #2	Teacher #3

.com			
.gif, .bmp, .jpg			
.gov			
.org			
3-D			
Alignment			
Background/foreground			
Clone			
Color palette			
Crop			
Ctrl+click			
Data			
Design gallery			
Desk top publishing			
Doc			
Drill down			
Export			
F keys			
Formula			
Handles			
Html			
Hyperlink			
Netiquette			
Network			
Pixels			
Scheme			
Screen shot			
Screen print			
Select-do			
Taskbar			
Toggle			
Tooltip			
Tri-fold			
Washout			
Website address			
WYSIWYG			
Y axis			

Speak Like a Geek Grading

Name: _____

Class: _____

WORD DEFINED:_____

Eye contact _____

Knew word _____

Knew definition _____

Used word in sentence _____

Sentence showed student knew the definition _____

Audience could help if necessary _____

Presence _____

Vocal (no um's, slang, 'something', 'stuff', etc.) _____

Overall _____

EXCEL QUIZ

FIFTH GRADE EXCEL QUIZ

1	Read all directions first
2	Be sure to enter information in the correction location (see Column C for locations)
3	If you get stuck, move on to the next step
4	When you're finished, try the Extra Credit

Location	Skill
A1	Enter title 'Fifth Grade Skills--font size 26; Merge-center over A1-F1
	rename the worksheet tab 'quiz review'
	recolor the 'quiz review' tab
A2	Your name--font size 10, font colored red
A3	Your teacher's name; font comic sans
A4	The date, using keyboard shortcut
F1-J6	Insert any picture
	resize Row 3 and Column D
A6-C10	Enter the data and labels to the right
	Include shading and border
	Make a chart from data (step 9); add a title and the X and Y labels
A12-E21	Color row 5 and row 11 blue
	Type the table below, including all data; use Excel formulas to find the answers

Extra Credit

Step 8: format table (change bars, colors, background)

Put a border around either table

Turn the picture into a hyperlink to your file folder

Add text 'Click Here for Falconer'

Subject	boys	girls
Arts	5	3
LA	0	0
Math	6	8
Science	1	0

Sample only -- yours will be on a separate worksheet

Addition	Subtract	Multiply	Divide
44	123	33	144
32	33	66	12

Average
22
33
44
55
66
77
77
88

Lesson #21—Google Earth Tour

Vocabulary	Problem solving	Collaborations
☐ *Google Earth* ☐ *Placemark* ☐ *Tour* ☐ *Wonders of World*	☐ *My program disappeared* ☐ *The link doesn't work (copy-paste into address bar)* ☐ *How do I play GE tour?*	☐ *Social studies* ☐ *Problem solving* ☐ *Science* ☐ *Geography*
NETS-S Standards: *3. Research and information; 5. Digital citizenship*		

Lesson questions? Go to http://askatechteacher.com

Type to Learn or online keyboarding websites

_____ Correct posture; Correct hand position—curved over home row; elbows at sides

Speak Like a Geek presentations start today. Demonstrate how and let students begin

Lesson Plan: Students create a tour on Google Earth using locations selected by the classroom teacher or sites used for the Google Earth Board. They placemark the locations, add a fact, and add them to a tour file folder in Google Earth. This is popular with students and fun to see the most amazing parts of our globe.

_____ Remind students how to take a tour (remember 3rd and 4th grade tours?). Take tours create by last year's fifth graders. Notice how locations are in the same file folder and how the tour goes in order

_____ Discuss Google Earth's top toolbar, left sidebar with search/places/Layers. Explain 'fly to' field; explain locations under 'My Places'; explain layers (make sure 3D Buildings and Street View are on)

_____ Make a file folder under 'Places' called 'My Tour' with student name

_____ Type student's home into 'fly to' bar and visit. Placemark this as first location. Customize by using student picture as placemark. This lets us see all student tour locations by identifying his/her unique placemark. Add a fact about student to dialogue box. Make sure placemarks end up under 'My Tour'. If not, cut and paste into folder.

_____ 2nd location: Mark school with customized placemark.

_____ Mark eight locations covered in Google Earth Board wonders of the world in the same manner (see list below) and add each location to 'My Tour' with one fact about each learned from presentations (see sample list from my student presentations.

_____ Save tour.

> Compaq is considering changing the command "Press Any Key" to "Press Return Key" because of the many calls asking where the "Any" key is.

GOOGLE EARTH PROJECT

- Find ten locations on Google Earth. These must include:
    - *Your house*
    - *Your school*
    - *8 locations from the list below*
- Use Google Earth Community for hard-to-find locations
- Create a file folder under 'My Places' called '***'s Tour'
- Save all locations to your folder
    - *Pick a unique placemark*
    - *Fill in placemark name and info*
    - *Add one fact about the location*

Some Locations for Google Earth Project Tour

Egyptian Pyramids	Death Valley
Stonehenge	Straits of Gibraltar
Leaning Tower of Pisa	Mt. St. Helens
Panama Canal	Great African Rift
Victoria Falls	Istanbul
Mt. Everest	Madagascar
The Ross Ice Shelf	Siberia
San Andreas Fault	Suez Canal
Great Wall of China	Taj Mahal
The Red Sea	The Eiffel Tower
Tierra del Fuego	Ngorongoro Crater
Ayers Rock	Hagia Sophia, Istanbul

WONDERS OF GOOGLE EARTH TOUR FACTS

LOCATION	INTERESTING FACTS
Ayers Rock	❖ One of the oldest rocks on Earth. ❖ Perimeter is 5 miles ❖ Has a waterfall called Alice Sprints ❖ Changes colors depending upon the time of day
Death Valley	❖ Record for highest temperature in the Western hemisphere—134 degrees ❖ Second hottest recorded temperature in the world ❖ Lowest spot in North America at 282 feet below sea level
Egyptian Pyramids	❖ Pyramid features are so large they can be seen from the Moon ❖ The oldest structures in existence ❖ They are oriented north-south ❖ There are around 110 Egyptian pyramids
Eiffel Tower	❖ Built in 1887; completed in 1889 for the World Fair ❖ 324 meters tall, out of 9441 tons of wrought iron ❖ Repainted every 7 years; requires 50 tons of brown paint in 3 shades, darkest at bottom ❖ More than 200,000 people visited it during the World's Fair of 1889
Great African Rift	❖ Named by a 19th century Brit explorer named John Walter Gregory ❖ 3700 miles long, extending from Jordan to South Africa ❖ Site of the oldest human remains (3.7 million year old Lucy)
Great Wall of China	❖ …isn't a continuous wall. Stretches 4,000 miles ❖ Guarded by 2-3million soldiers ❖ Built 2,000 years ago by first emperor of China; rebuilt many times
Hagia Sophia, Istanbul	❖ 'Hagia Sophia' means the church of the hold wisdom in Greek ❖ One of several great churches built by Constantine the Great in the 4th Century ❖ Started as a patriarchal basilica, became a mosque and is now a museum
Istanbul	❖ First known as Byzantium and then Constantinople, now third largest city in the world ❖ Use to be the capital of the East Roman Empire and the Ottoman Empire ❖ Located in Turkey, its main religion is Islam
Leaning Tower of Pisa	❖ Took 177 years to build; started 1173 ❖ 55.86 m tall on one side and 56.7 m tall on the other; weighs about 14,500 tons ❖ Took 70 tons of dirt to stabilize the tower in May, 2008 ❖ It has 294 steps
Madagascar	❖ Island created when it separated from India 80-100 million years ago ❖ 4th largest island in the world ❖ No lions, giraffes, zebras, hippos here ❖ Home to 5% of the world's plants and animals
Mt. Everest	❖ Started growing about 60 million years ago ❖ 4000 people have attempted to climb it, but only 660 have succeeded. ❖ 142 people have died attempting to climb Mt. Everest ❖ Rises a few millimeters each year due to geologic forces
Mt. St. Helens	❖ An active volcano in the Cascade range in the state of Washington ❖ It is young for a volcano, only about 40,000 years old ❖ Last erupted in May 18, 1980, 8:32 am, for 9 hours. Killed 57 people, destroyed 250 homes, 47 bridges, 15 miles of railway and 185 miles of highway
Ngorongoro	❖ a haven for thousands of East African wild animals—lions, elephants, wildebeests ❖ The crater of an extinct volcano ❖ The area around the crater was occupied by early man 3 million years ago

Crater	
Panama Canal	❖ Man-made passage across Panama that connects Pacific and Atlantic Oceans ❖ Started by the French and finished by the Americans ❖ One of the largest and most difficult engineering projects ever undertaken
Red Sea	❖ Created from the movement of tectonic plates over 3 million years ago ❖ One of the most saline bodies of water in the world ❖ More than 1100 species of fish live here—10% of them found nowhere else
Ross Ice Shelf	❖ About the size of France with 90% of the floating ice below the water's surface ❖ Twice the size of Delaware ❖ Largest ice shelf in Antarctica, sits about 50 meters high from the water ❖ James Clark Ross discovered it in 1841 ❖ Ice Shelves are permanent floating ice sheets attached to land, fed by glaciers ❖ It has disintegrated and reappeared many times in the past
San Andreas Fault	❖ Land along the fault moves about 2 in. a year, about as fast as fingernails grow ❖ Located 800 miles along the length of California, beginning by the Salton Sea and extending to San Francisco bay ❖ Renowned as future cause of the 'Big One'—earthquake that will tear California apart
Siberia	❖ Takes up 77% of Russia's land and only 30% of its population ❖ The vast region covering almost all of northern Asia, now under Russian control ❖ The Soviet Union (no longer a nation) operated a series of labor camps here during the mid-1900's, for millions of political refugees, making 'Siberia' synonymous with exile and punishment
Stonehenge	❖ Blocks weighed as much as 4 tons and moved as far as 240 miles ❖ Built around 2500 b.c. ❖ Not actually a henge—based on construction
Straits of Gibraltar	❖ 22 miles wide ❖ The strait that separates Spain from Morocco ❖ Closed about 6 million years ago and reopened a million years later
Suez Canal	❖ Canal is 26 feet deep ❖ Opened in November, 1869 ❖ Opened in 1869, it is owned by an Egyptian company
Taj Mahal	❖ 5th of the 7 Wonders of the World ❖ Built by the Muslim Emperor Shah Jahan in memory of his wife ❖ Took 22 years to make
Tierra del Fuego	❖ Tierra del Fuego is Spanish for "Land of Fire" ❖ is an archipelago along the west side of South America, along the southernmost tip of the continent to the Strait of Magellan and Cape Horn ❖ the main island of the archipelago is also called Tierra del Fuego
Victoria Falls	❖ Twice the height of Niagara Falls ❖ Called the "Smoke that Thunders ❖ Makes the largest curtain of water in the world ❖ 1 mile wide; 360 feet tall

Google Earth Tour
Grading Rubric

*Your name:*_____

*Teacher:*_____

- **GE Tour**   ___ 1 points ___
  - ○ *File folder has student name*   _____
  - ○ *Tour runs*   _____

- **10 Placemarks**   ___ 15 points ___
  - ○ *Includes home*   _____
  - ○ *Include school*   _____
  - ○ *Includes 8 geographic locations from GE Bd.* _____
  - ○ *Each location includes a fact*   _____

- **Each Placemark…**   ___ 3 points ___
  - ○ *Placed correctly (geographically)*   _____
  - ○ *Labeled correctly (with location name)* _____
  - ○ *Customized with student picture*   _____

- **Overall Professional Look**   ___ 1 points ___

Student self-grading comments:

_____

_____

_____

_____.

Lesson #22—Graphics in Word I

Vocabulary	Problem solving	Collaborations
☐ Text box ☐ Print preview ☐ Crop ☐ Macro ☐ Format ☐ Washout	☐ My project disappeared (use search tool under Start button) ☐ Save early, save often ☐ How do I put a color block behind my pictures? (insert-picture-autoshape-basic shape; fill with paint bucket)	☐ Graphics design ☐ Art ☐ Critical thinking

NETS-S Standards:
1. Creativity and innovation; 6. Technology concepts

Lesson questions? Go to http://askatechteacher.com

Type to Learn or online keyboard websites

_____ Correct posture—centered in front of keyboard, legs in front, elbows at side

_____ Correct hand position—on home row, curved over keys, pointers on f and j

Speak Like a Geek presentations continue.

Keyboard Homework—remember to complete monthly

Lesson Plan: Teach basic photo-editing skills (borders, backgrounds, transparencies, fills, rotate, cropping) using only MS Word tools. Great for school projects and to introduce Photoshop

_____ Open Word; add heading (use macro—Alt+Shift+H) left aligned

_____ Insert row graphic from file folder provided in network folder (see samples below)

_____ Copy picture until there are as many copies as there are image parts (i.e., 5 copies of the ducks)

_____ Use crop tool to crop each part (i.e., duck or house) as a separate picture

_____ Select one picture, then click 'Picture tools' at top of screen. Format picture (add border, backgrounds, etc) using ribbon toolbar. Use green dot at top of picture to rotate the image. Make each one different.

_____ Print Preview before printing to be sure it fits on one page

_____ Save to your file folder; close to desktop for next week

Problem solving: If your screen freezes:

☐ *"Smash forehead on keyboard to continue..."*

☐ *"Enter any 11-digit prime number to continue..."*

WORD PICTURE MANIPULATION

1. Copy-paste the row graphic above to a new Word document.
2. Put a dog in front of the little girl

3. Copy the row five times and paste onto page
4. Crop each person out
5. Change background
6. Add a border around picture
7. Turn one of the pictures into a watermark
8. Rotate several of the pictures

Lesson #23—Graphics in Word II

Vocabulary	Problem solving	Collaborations
☐ *Format* ☐ *Fill* ☐ *Print preview* ☐ *Crop* ☐ *Border* ☐ *Wpm*	☐ *I can't close (Alt+F4)* ☐ *What's today's date (Shift+Alt+D)* ☐ *My program disappeared (check the taskbar)* ☐ *My typing disappeared (Ctrl+Z)*	☐ *Graphic design* ☐ *Science* ☐ *Humanities* ☐ *History*

NETS-S Standards:
1. Creativity and innovation; 6. Technology concepts

Lesson questions? Go to http://askatechteacher.com

Type to Learn or online keyboarding website (see appendix for ideas)

_____ Correct posture—centered in front of computer, legs in front

_____ Correct hand position—both hands on home row, curved fingers

_____ Go to TypingWeb.com (http://www.typingtest.com/). Take three-minute speed quiz. How are you doing? This program deducts wpm for mistakes. Notice speed and accuracy; take a second speed test. If there were more than five mistakes on the first test, slow down to improve accuracy. If there were less than five mistakes, push to type faster. Students know where the keys are. After the second speed quiz, shut the program down.

Speak Like a Geek presentations continue

Graphics manipulation—prepare students for Photoshop

_____ Open project begun last week. Finish placing a border around each cropped picture and changing background of each; rotate them with the green dot

_____ Go to 'Print preview' before printing—be sure everything fits on one page. Resize as needed

_____ Print (Ctrl+P); save (Ctrl+S); save-as to flash drive

Done? Create a holiday card in KidPix with skills learned in K-2. No assistance required

_____ Open KidPix and create a card (skills learned in K-2 so this is student-directed)

_____ Use paint brush, paint bucket and text tool. Save and print when done.

Titanic Virus:
Your computer goes down.
Alzheimer Virus:
Your computer forgets where it put your files.
Child Virus:
Your computer constantly does annoying things, but is too cute to get rid of.
Disney Virus:
Everything in your computer goes Goofy

HAPPY ST. PATRICK'S DAY

Lesson #24—Photoshop I—Cropping

Vocabulary	Problem solving	Collaborations
☐ Pixels ☐ Macro ☐ Transform ☐ Scale ☐ Inverse ☐ Crop	☐ I can't get to my picture (check layers) ☐ How do I undo (go to history) ☐ I'm drawing but nothing's happening (are you in the right layer?)	☐ Art ☐ Critical thinking

NETS-S Standards:
1. Creativity and innovation; 4. Critical thinking; 5. Digital citizenship

Lesson questions? Go to http://askatechteacher.com

Type to Learn or online keyboarding website—correct hand position, body posture
Speak Like a Geek—continue presentations
Review problem solving using examples above or others from problem-solving board

Lesson plan: Introduce Photoshop. Show three ways to crop and when you would select each. Have students select pictures they'll be using for a class project or one of themselves to practice this skill.

_____ Introduce Photoshop (or the free version called Gimp)—review layout, basics, toolbars, zoom in on pixels, history, layers, navigator. Option: Use the free download Gimp (http://www.gimp.org/) . It's similar to Photoshop. Let students know Adobe has wonderful discounts on its software for students

_____ Open a picture. Use auto correction tools under image-adjustments (auto levels/contrast/color). Point out 'History' (on right). Compare the original picture to the corrected version to see the difference. It's impressive.

_____ Point out the crop tool with the dark arrow in corner (opens to two tools), the lasso and the magic wand. Explain what cropping is and how each of these tools does it differently.

_____ Try the crosshatch crop tool and the lasso on a new picture. Notice the difference—one is structured, one freehand. Compare the three approaches to cropping in MS Word.

_____ Now use magic wand to crop out a background (i.e., the lizard below). Open a background (i.e., the coliseum below). Drag-drop the cropped-out figure into the new background

_____ Use edit-transform-scale to resize picture into background

Save; save-as to flash drive. Close down to desktop

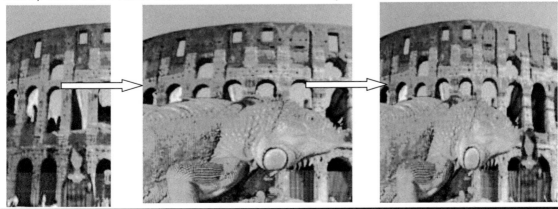

Lesson #25—Photoshop II

Vocabulary	Problem solving	Collaborations
☐ Clone	☐ How do I print? (Ctrl+P)	☐ Art
☐ Anchor point	☐ My shift key doesn't work? (Is caps	☐ Desktop publishing
☐ Filter	lock on?)	☐ Critical thinking
☐ .psd	☐ How do I undo? (go to history)	
☐ .jpg	☐ My toolbars disappeared	

NETS-S Standards:
1. Creativity and innovation; 4. Critical thinking; 5. Digital citizenship

Lesson questions? Go to http://askatechteacher.com

Type to Learn or online typing program

_____ Correct posture—body centered in front of keyboard

_____ Correct hand position—both hands curved over home row

Speak Like a Geek—continue presentations

Lesson plan: Using Photoshop, add or subtract features from a pictures (i.e., polar bears); clone from one picture to another. Use this skill to support a classroom unit of inquiry, or to teach about ethical issues (because cloning looks authentic)

_____ Open Photoshop (or Gimp). Discuss cloning and the clone tool.

Open a field of flowers (see inset below). Show students how to clone within a picture. Add flowers or get rid of flowers by cloning the flowers or the green verdure.

Show how to watch the anchor point to see where you're cloning from, to make colors match as closely as possible.

_____ You can also clone between two pictures. Open Sub and Polar Bear picture (or similar—see sample on next page) and a second picture (like the sea cave). Create anchor point with Alt+click in one picture (the Arctic ice flow) and paint with mouse to clone a polar bear to a Caribbean sea cave. Notice the cross shows where you're cloning from.

_____ Make sure edges are matched as closely as possible to look as natural as possible. Be patient.

_____ Use the camera on the history button to keep a copy of a stage in the picture you like. Explain to students how this works.

_____ Save to file folder as both a .psd (Photoshop's default file. It will keep all the layers for later editing) and a .jpg (a file that will be usable in many programs and the internet)

Add flowers

Delete flowers

Start with a picture with a focal point you like. Duplicate it or add it to a new background:

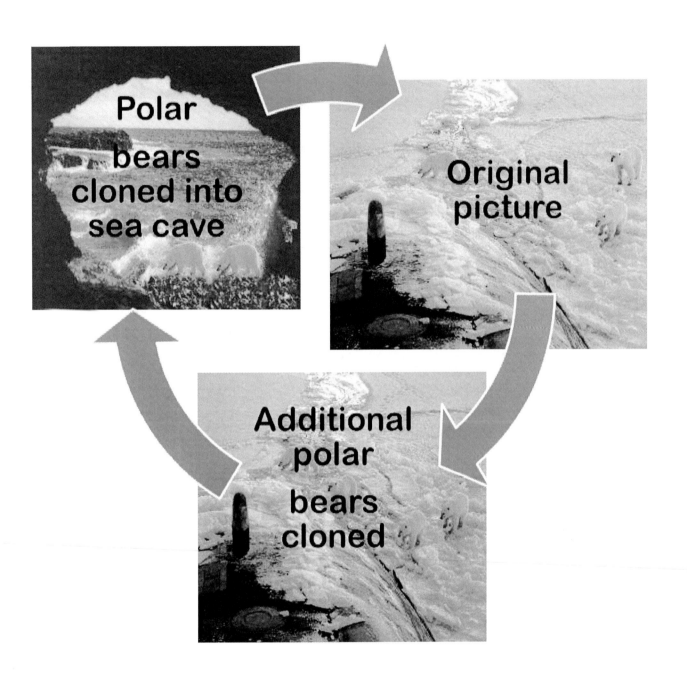

Lesson #26—Photoshop III

Vocabulary	Problem solving	Collaborations
☐ Warp ☐ Magic wand ☐ Background ☐ Foreground ☐ Color palette	☐ I can't find my project (did you back it up?) ☐ The computer didn't save my project (Did you save to 'My Documents' by accident?)	☐ Art ☐ Critical thinking ☐ Desktop publishing
<u>NETS-S Standards:</u> 1. Creativity and innovation; 4. Critical thinking; 5. Digital citizenship		

<u>Lesson questions? Go to http://askatechteacher.com</u>

Keyboard—Type to Learn or online keyboarding website
_____   Correct posture—body in front of keyboard, hands curved over home row
_____   Remember to turn in homework
Speak Like a Geek—continue presentations

Lesson plan: Work with Photoshop filters. There are dozens that add texture and overlays to images. Let students loose to be as creative as they want. Discuss how each brings out a different emotion or meaning to finished product. Add text and custom brushes for pizazz.

_____   Open school picture (or other). Use Photoshop's magic wand to delete background (or adapt to use Gimp).
_____   Change background and foreground colors. I've selected pink and maroon
_____   Filter-render-clouds to replace background with clouds shaded to these two colors
_____   Select inverse (now ants are moving around the person). Filter.
_____   Use text tool to add a holiday greeting—change font, size, color, and warp
_____   Use paint brush to spray stars or other touches
_____   Save as jpg. Print with preview—check box to fit picture to medium.

Lesson #27—Photoshop IV

Vocabulary	Problem solving	Collaborations
☐ *Toolbar* ☐ *History tab* ☐ *Actions tab*	☐ *Program disappeared (check taskbar)* ☐ *My hyperlink doesn't work (try Ctrl+click)*	☐ *Art* ☐ *Photography*
NETS-S Standards: *1. Creativity and innovation; 4. Critical thinking; 5. Digital citizenship*		

Lesson questions? Go to http://askatechteacher.com

Keyboard—Type to Learn or online keyboard site

_____ Correct posture—body centered in front of keyboard

Speak Like a Geek—continue presentations

Lesson plan: Use Adobe Photoshop Actions, history brush and artistic filters for a creative rendition of your favorite picture. These are simple effects that add a sophisticated look, i.e., frames, quadrant colors, textures, image effects. This is a fun addition to a Photoshop unit.

_____ Open giraffe picture or other of your choice (see left inset below) or use the free Gimp with some adaptations.

_____ Use blur tool on tool bar to blur trees in background. This is a common effect used to make a focal point stand out in a picture. Show samples from magazines that students will recognize.

_____ Return to original picture in history and try the same thing with the smudge tool

_____ Return to original picture using history. Go to 'Actions' (next to 'History'). Walk students through the many different 'Actions' Photoshop has available. Explain that these are popular but complicated multi-step formatting effects that Photoshop has automated to make simple to use.

_____ Select 'Image Effects, Quadrant Colors'; push 'go' at bottom to create a four-color picture (see middle example below).

_____ Go to 'Frames, Brushed Aluminum' under 'Actions'; push 'go' button and watch a frame appear around the picture. Recolor the frame with the Styles tab

_____ Return to original picture; select 'fresco' under 'Filter-Artistic' to filter the image

_____ Select 'History brush tool' from left toolbar. Anchor 'history' to the original picture. This sets what the brush 'paints back' to. Paint over giraffe to bring back the original giraffe while background retains 'Fresco' look (see right inset below)

_____ These four tools are simple to learn and stunning in the effect on a picture.

Save to file folder and flash drive; close down to desktop

Lesson #28—Photoshop V

Vocabulary	Problem solving	Collaborations
☐ Foreground ☐ Background ☐ Task pane ☐ Paint bucket ☐ Gradient tool ☐ Fill ☐ Styles ☐ Canvas ☐ Layers ☐ Variegated	☐ My picture got weird (only use corner handles) ☐ My headphones don't work (are they plugged in?) ☐ I'm painting but nothing is happening (are you in right layer?) ☐ My Styles layer won't show (Are you in a new layer and the paint bucket?) ☐ I can't edit the text (are you in the text layer?)	☐ Art ☐ Desktop publishing ☐ Critical thinking
NETS-S Standards: 1. Creativity and innovation; 4. Critical thinking; 5. Digital citizenship		

Lesson questions? Go to http://askatechteacher.com

Type to Learn or online keyboard site—see appendix for examples

_____ Correct posture—legs in front of body, body in front of keyboard

_____ Correct hand position—curved over home row

Speak Like a Geek—continue presentations

Lesson Plan: Experiment with backgrounds. Try different paint brushes, tools, and custom shapes. Put everything on a canvas and see what comes out. Because of the blend of structure and free-flow, this is popular with all types of students.

_____ Open new canvas in Photoshop (or Gimp).

_____ Try different backgrounds using 1) background/foreground color, 2) styles, 3) gradient, 4) pattern

_____ Create a new layer. Double click its name and rename it 'background'. Change foreground and background colors on the left tool bar to new colors. Select Paint Bucket. Make sure 'fill' on top tool bar says 'foreground'. Use paint bucket to pour a layer. It will be the color of the foreground that was selected.

_____ Create a second layer. Name it Patterns. Select the paint bucket; this time, make sure 'fill' says 'pattern' and select a pattern from the drop down box. Pour it onto the new layer.

_____ Open a third layer. Rename it 'styles'. Select the paint bucket, and then select a style (on right). Pour the style onto the new layer. Don't like it? Pour a new one. Don't want a style anymore? Click the paint bucket and pour. It'll be the foreground color.

_____ Create a fourth layer and name it 'Gradient'. Select gradient tool under paint bucket. Drag mouse across screen to create a variegated background.

_____ Have students drag their favorite background layer to the top of the stack.

_____ Add a new layer. Use paint brush to draw on it; use Custom shapes to add pizzazz. Use text to tell classmates what's going on.

_____ Save as a .psd and a .jpg

Close down to desktop (Alt+F4); say yes to save

Use custom shapes and all types of paint brushes. Want more brushes? Append them from Photoshop's library.

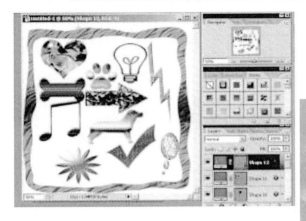

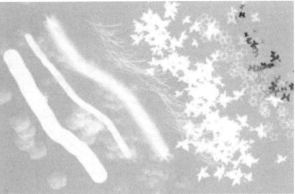

Sum up this lesson with a background, custom shapes and text (add paint too if you'd like)

Lesson #29—Hello to Next Year's Students

Vocabulary	Problem solving	Collaborations
☐ *Tagxedo* ☐ *Trading card* ☐ *Screen shot* ☐ *Word picture* ☐ *.jpg*	☐ *I can't find my project (check file folder, My Documents and backup flash drive)* ☐ *I can't figure this out (try help files)*	☐ *Critical thinking skills* ☐ *Problem-solving skills* ☐ *Music*
NETS-S Standards: *1. Creativity and innovation; 4. Critical thinking, problem solving*		

Lesson questions? Go to http://askatechteacher.com

Type to Learn or online keyboarding sites. Watch posture
Speak Like a Geek—continue presentations
Sum up this year and have students share their thoughts with next year's fifth graders.

_____ Remember Tagxedos from fourth grade? Create a Tagxedo with 50 words that describe this year to incoming fifth graders. (see two samples on next page)

_____ Have <u>Tagxedo</u> website available on <u>class internet start page</u>

_____ Follow directions on website for adding text and formatting the image.

_____ Have students add at least fifty words that describe what they did this year, what they liked, didn't like, found challenging, found easy, will remember and use, will never use again. The more significant the word, the more often it should be entered so it will come out bigger on the Tagxedo.

_____ Take a screen shot of the word picture and save as a .jpg.

_____ Next, students will use <u>Big Huge Labs</u> to create a trading card of themselves with a paragraph of their hints to incoming fifth graders. These can be laminated and mounted on the wall or a bulletin board to greet new students.

_____ Go to <u>Big Huge Labs</u> (http://bighugelabs.com/). Select Trading Card project (see inset below).

_____ Use school picture taken at beginning of year. Pick a background. Title is student name. Subtitle is an enthusiastic greeting to new students. Description is thoughts on 5th grade technology—good, bad, hints, favorites, things to avoid. Add icons to decorate trading card and create.

_____ Save; print so it's ¼ size on 8.5x11 paper.

Close down to desktop; save

"A computer is like an Old Testament God, with a lot of rules and no mercy."

Tagxedo built from words on Class Start Page

Tagxedo based on hints from this year's fifth graders to next year's group:

A Note to My Readers : How I Use Web 2.0 Tools in My Classroom to Communicate with Parents

I've been teaching for over twenty years in different schools, different communities, but one factor transcends grades, classes, and culture: Parents want to be involved with what's going on at their children's school. Parent-teacher communication is vital and in my experience, the number one predictor of success for a student. But parents can't always get in to the classroom as a volunteer and see what's written on the white board. They can't always make the school meetings to hear the comings and goings of the school. Why? It's not lack of interest. More likely, they're working; doing that 8-5 thing that insures the future of their families and pays for their children's college education.

Knowing the importance of parent involvement, I feel that my job as a teacher includes not just the lessons I share with students but keeping my parents informed on classroom happenings. I need to be as transparent as possible, get as much information as I can out to parents in a manner they can understand and a format they can access. If I could tape my classes and post them on YouTube, or offer a live feed during class, I would. But I can't, so I try other creative ideas.

Class website
This is teacher directed, but gives me a chance to communicate class activities, pictures, homework, and extra credit opportunities–all the little details that make up a class–with parents. This is a first stop to understanding what's going on in class.

Class wiki
This is student-directed, student-centered. Students post summaries of their tech class, examples of their work, projects they've completed on the wiki for everyone to share. This way, parents see the class through the eyes of the students. And so do I, which is my way of assuring that what I think happened, did.

Twitter
I love tweets because they're quick, 140 character summaries of activities, announcements, events. They take no time to read and are current.

Emails
I send lots of these out with reminders, updates, FAQs, discussion of issues that are confusing to parents. I often ask if I'm sending too many, but my parents insist they love them.

Open door
I'm available every day after school, without an appointment. Because I have so many other ways to stay in touch, my classroom rarely gets so crowded that I can't deal with everyone on a personal level.

Lesson #30—What Have I Learned I

Vocabulary	Problem solving	Collaborations
☐ *Critical thinking* ☐ *Problem-solving* ☐ *Help files* ☐ *Upload*	☐ *My computer doesn't work (is the power on?)* ☐ *My monitor doesn't work (is the power on?)*	☐ *Music* ☐ *Language* ☐ *Critical-thinking skills* ☐ *Problem-solving skills*

<u>NETS-S Standards:</u>
1. Creativity and innovation; 4. Decision making

Lesson questions? Go to http://askatechteacher.com

Keyboard—Type to Learn or one of the online keyboarding sites

_____ Correct posture—body centered in front of keyboard

_____ Correct hand position—hands curved over home row

Speak Like a Geek—finish presentations today. Anyone who hasn't gone, will today

Lesson Plan—Critical-thinking skills—try new programs. Technology class isn't about learning how to use programs. It's how to think at a computer. What are taskbars and toolbars? How does one get started—figure out the tricks of a program? These skills cut across the boundaries of software and websites and are about the student's ability to think critically and problem-solve. Let's see if that has happened this year.

_____ Open PrintMusic program (or a program your students haven't used this year)

_____ How does one start? Is there a tutorial or a demo? Is there a Help button? How did we initiate other programs we used this year?

_____ Figure out how to create a new composition. How did we open a new Word doc? A new Photoshop canvas? Select instruments you are familiar with; compose music for a fifth grade graduation ceremony

_____ Add notes, articulations, dynamics, rests. Add lyrics to complement the music—be sure they go along with the rhythm and notes

_____ Save to file folder; print for teacher

_____ Advanced: Visit PrintMusic's website—www.finalemusic.com

Here, you can download/upload music that others have composed using PrintMusic—see what peers have done.

Lesson #31—What Have I Learned II

Vocabulary	Problem solving	Collaborations
☐ *Tutorial*	☐ *My screen froze (Is there a dialogue box open?)*	☐ *Design*
☐ *Floor plan*	☐ *Can't exit program (try Alt+F4)*	☐ *Architecture*
☐ *Map*		☐ *Critical thinking*
☐ *Template*	☐ *How do I use a link in a document (Ctrl+click)*	☐ *Problem solving*
☐ *Drag-and-drop*	☐ *How do I get help? (F2)*	
☐ *Jeopardy*	☐ *I don't understand this program (is it like another you do understand?)*	
☐ *Critical thinking*		
☐ *Problem solving*		

NETS-S Standards:
1. Creativity and innovation; 4. Problem solving

Lesson questions? Go to http://askatechteacher.com

Type to Learn or an online keyboarding website

_____ Correct posture—body centered in front of keyboard

Critical-thinking skills—teach independence as they use programs they are not trained in.

_____ Students can work in pairs for this exercise.

_____ Open Microsoft Visio. Go to the Help files—Getting Started Tutorial. Need more help? Try YouTube videos (with teacher supervision) or Google a specific problem.

_____ Spend as much time as possible going through these help locations

_____ Visio project: Create a map showing how to go from the school to student's house and partner's house. Done? Create a floor plan showing inside of houses

_____ Experiment with drawing types, shapes, resizing, etc.

_____ Add text for titles, labels and names

_____ Save; print

Dry run of next week's challenge (see instructions under Lesson #32)

_____ End of Year Challenge includes questions compiled from a year's worth of tech classes presented in a Jeopardy-style game. Students challenge each other for extra credit, free dress passes, whatever the prize du jour is. It is a fun way to review what they've learned and encourage them to study.

_____ Have them decide how their team will prepare for the Team Challenge. Give them 15-20 minutes to do this.

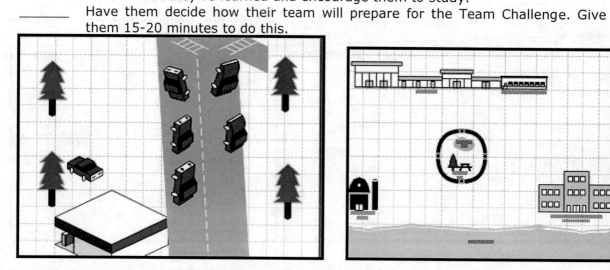

Lesson #32—End-of-Year Team Challenge

Vocabulary	Problem solving	Collaborations
Tutorial *Help files* *Drawing* *Resizing* *Category*	*How do I _____? (try Help files)* *How do I use this program? (Is there a demo or help files?)* *How do I save/print? (try the way you did it in other programs)*	☐ *Architecture* ☐ *Critical thinking*
NETS-S Standards: *3. Research and information fluency; 6. Technology concepts*		

Lesson questions? Go to http://askatechteacher.com

Lesson Plan: Team Challenge. This is a list of questions compiled from a year's worth of tech classes. I use them in a Jeopardy-style game at the end of the year. Students create teams and challenge each other for extra credit, free dress passes, whatever the prize du jour is. It is a fun way to review what they've learned and encourage them to study.

_____ Put students into teams. Remind them about last week's practice. Who prepared? Who practiced? Pass out list of categories—not questions (see next pages) to students.

_____ Have one student be time keeper (if none wants to, you can do it).

_____ Team #1 selects a category. Ask a question within that category (see list on next pages). Give team 5-10 seconds to answer. If they can't answer, proceed to Team #2, but don't repeat the question. If they don't know the question or can't answer, move on to Team #3 and then Team #4. If no one can answer, provide the answer (because they'll be curious by now)

_____ Next category selection goes to Team #2—even if they were the ones who answered Team #1's question. This is how teams get ahead of competitors. (Be sure to keep records—it's the most oft-disputed part of this game in my classes!) Pose question to them from the selected category and repeat step above.

_____ Each team gets to select the category their question will come from. Ask each question only once. Each category is selected only once. This insurers students can't always go back to an 'easy' section

_____ Go around class so each group has an opportunity to have first crack at a category/question. Notice where groups have difficulties and remind yourself to concentrate more on these next year.

_____ Prizes? Optional. I give Free passes that include sitting where student wants, skip a homework, 5 extra credit points—prizes I know they value and will get them excited. You might decide to have no prizes.

_____ Extra: Put this into a real Jeopardy template (see appendix for sites)

Done? Students can go to Big Site of Great Kids Websites (http://askatechteacher.wordpress.com/great-websites-for-kids/)—this is my collection of all websites they've visited this year. You can develop your own!

"The box said, WinXP or better required... so I used a Mac!"

END-OF-YEAR TEAM CHALLENGE

Review the following concepts. These are the questions that will be asked during the Team Challenge—to find the semester's most tech-savvy student!

Word Skills

- Why use Word?
- When do you use Word for schoolwork?
- What does the red squiggly line mean
- How do you clear a red squiggly line
- What does green squiggly line mean
- How do you clear a green squiggly line
- How do you change image background?
- How do you insert a page border
- How do you resize a picture
- How do you insert an autoshape
- How do you add color to an autoshape
- How do you add a text box

- How do you add a toolbar to your Word
- How do you spell-check a document?
- What is a call-out box?
- How do you add a call-out box to a document?
- How do you make a macro in Word?
- How do you add a watermark?
- How do you add a footer
- How do you double-space
- How do you insert WordArt
- How do you add a border

KEYBOARD SHORTCUTS

- →
- ☺
- Print (Ctrl+P)
- Save (Ctrl+S)
- Copy (Ctrl+C)
- Paste (Ctrl+V)
- Undo (Ctrl+Z)
- Bold (Ctrl+B)
- Italics (Ctrl+I)
- Underline (Ctrl+U)
- Zoom in on a webpage (Ctrl++)

- Zoom out of a webpage (Ctrl+-)
- Exit a program (Alt+F4)
- Insert the current date (Shift+Alt+D)
- Insert the current time (Shift+Alt+T)
- Help (F1)
- New page (Ctrl+Enter)
- Make a graph in Excel (F11)
- Bring back internet toolbar (F11)
- Toggle between taskbar tasks (Alt+tab)

Vocabulary

- Back-up
- Clip art
- Shortcut
- Cursor
- Desktop
- Recycle bin
- Hour glass
- Icon
- Floppy disk
- Folder
- Mouse over
- Task bar
- Drop down menu
- Format
- Font
- Queue
- Handles
- Toolbar
- Scrollbar
- Wizard
- Multimedia

- Explorer
- PC
- Netiquette
- Footer
- Thesaurus
- Page Break
- Hyperlink
- Active window
- I-beam
- Initialize
- Dialogue box
- Kilobyte
- Pixel
- Search engine
- Browser
- Thumbnail
- Tile
- Drill down
- Right-click menu
- Log-on
- Protocol

- Alt
- F4
- Cc
- Win 7
- Caps lock
- Monitor
- Footer
- Animation
- Transition
- GIF
- JPG
- .com
- .edu
- .net
- .org
- Auto-play
- Auto-advance
- Place saver
- Bullets
- Numbered list
- Crop

- Print preview
- Washout
- Watermark
- Import
- Export
- Data
- Textbook
- Worksheet
- Default
- Internet address
- Network
- Back button
- Forward button
- Printkey
- Wrap
- Search bar
- Address bar
- Google (verb)
- Hits
- Synonym
- Flash drive

- USB port
- Jump drive
- Thumb drive
- Digital locker
- Upload

Lab Rules

- Name three lab rules
- How often should you save?
- How do you print from the internet?
- What does "Respect everyone's work" mean?
- When can you eat in the lab?
- What internet site can you go on?
- What is proper posture at the computer?
- When can you plagiarize?

- When do you not have to give credit for information from the internet?
- Who is to blame if you miss work or homework or forget your book?
- Which four letter words are specifically prohibited ('can't', 'won't')
- If you don't know a lab rule, does that mean you aren't responsible for following it?
- When is it OK to go into someone else's file folder?
- What if you miss a class?
- When can you touch someone else's equipment?

Problem Solving

- How do you save a document
- How do you print a document
- What is the name of the color printer
- What do you do if your monitor is black when you sit down
- What is the next thing you do if your monitor is black when you sit down
- What if your volume doesn't work
- What if your computer doesn't work
- What if your mouse doesn't work
- What's the right mouse button for

- How do you move between cells in Excel
- What is the password to log-on the computer
- What is the user name to log-on the computer
- How do you find the date on the computer
- What keyboard shortcut auto-inserts current date
- How do you search for a file
- What if your capitals are stuck on
- How do you fix a weird looking resized image
- What if F11 doesn't create the chart in Excel
- What's the keyboard shortcut to close a program
- If a double-click doesn't work, what do you do
- What if you accidentally delete words/pictures
- What do you do if your desktop icons are messed up
- What if your Start button disappears
- Name two things you do if your screen seems frozen

Internet

- How do you copy-paste from the internet
- How do you send an email from your home
- How do you request a Return Receipt for email
- What is a search engine
- What is the 'Back' button
- What is the 'Forward' button
- What is the 'Home' button
- What is the 'Refresh' button
- What's the difference between the search bar and the address bar
- What is the Address Bar

- What's the 'History' tool
- How to bookmark a site
- How to print (copy-paste to Word first)
- How do you add to Favorites
- What is Favorites
- When can you go on the internet at school
- Name one address we have visited on the internet
- How do you attach a document to an email
- How do you select the best site from a search engine

Publisher

- How do you insert a page
- How do you add text
- What is 'Design Gallery'
- What is the 'Task Pane'?
- How do you add a border

- How do you insert a picture
- How do you insert picture from KidPix
- How do you move material from one page to another

- Name four projects we did in Publisher
- How do you add a Table of Contents
- How do you add a footer
- Why use Publisher?

- How do you add the page number to the footer
- How do you enlarge a page

Graphics

- How do you crop a picture
- How do you change a picture background
- What is Photoshop
- How do you wrap text around a picture
- How do you resize a picture
- How do you move an image around page

- How do you insert from a file
- How do you insert from the internet
- How do you insert from clipart
- When you insert a clipart image, where does it go (the blinking cursor)

Windows

- How do you add a file folder to network?
- What can you do with a right-click?
- What is a right click?
- How do you know what programs you have open?
- How do you change the wallpaper?

- What if the taskbar is gone?
- What if the start button is gone?
- What are Function keys?
- Name something on a right click menu
- How do you toggle between tasks on taskbar

Basics

- How do you save
- What is the network file
- What is a local disk
- How do you print

- Name 5 parts of the computer
- How do you 'Print screen'

PowerPoint

- Why use PowerPoint
- How to add slides
- How to delete slides
- How to add animations
- How to add transitions
- How to add moving pictures
- How to add GIF's
- How to add sounds

- How to change background
- How to use pictures for backgrounds
- How to insert pictures from clipart
- How to insert pictures from the internet
- How to insert pictures from your home file folder
- How to insert hyperlinks
- How to auto-advance slides

Excel

- Why use Excel? How to enter data
- How to graph data
- How to alphabetize names
- How to auto-sum
- How to average numbers
- How to add numbers
- How to subtract numbers
- How to multiply numbers
- How to divide numbers

- How to widen columns
- How to widen rows
- How to format text
- How to insert a picture
- How to add the date
- How to add the time
- How to change the worksheet name
- How to change the tab color
- How to add a worksheet

The ISTE
National Educational Technology Standards

and Performance Indicators for Students

1. **Creativity and Innovation**
   Students demonstrate creative thinking, construct knowledge, and develop innovative products and processes using technology. Students:
   a. apply existing knowledge to generate new ideas, products, or processes.
   b. create original works as a means of personal or group expression.
   c. use models and simulations to explore complex systems and issues.
   d. identify trends and forecast possibilities.

2. **Communication and Collaboration**
   Students use digital media and environments to communicate and work collaboratively, including at a distance, to support individual learning and contribute to the learning of others. Students:
   a. interact, collaborate, and publish with peers, experts, or others employing a variety of digital environments and media.
   b. communicate information and ideas effectively to multiple audiences using a variety of media and formats.
   c. develop cultural understanding and global awareness by engaging with learners of other cultures.
   d. contribute to project teams to produce original works or solve problems.

3. **Research and Information Fluency**
   Students apply digital tools to gather, evaluate, and use information. Students:
   a. plan strategies to guide inquiry.
   b. locate, organize, analyze, evaluate, synthesize, and ethically use information from a variety of sources and media.
   c. evaluate and select information sources and digital tools based on the appropriateness to specific tasks.
   d. process data and report results.

4. **Critical Thinking, Problem Solving, and Decision Making**
   Students use critical thinking skills to plan and conduct research, manage projects, solve problems, and make informed decisions using appropriate digital tools and resources. Students:
   a. identify and define authentic problems and significant questions for investigation.
   b. plan and manage activities to develop a solution or complete a project.
   c. collect and analyze data to identify solutions and/or make informed decisions.
   d. use multiple processes and diverse perspectives to explore alternative solutions.

5. **Digital Citizenship**
   Students understand human, cultural, and societal issues related to technology and practice legal and ethical behavior. Students:
   a. advocate and practice safe, legal, and responsible use of information and technology.
   b. exhibit a positive attitude toward using technology that supports collaboration, learning, and productivity.
   c. demonstrate personal responsibility for lifelong learning.
   d. exhibit leadership for digital citizenship.

6. **Technology Operations and Concepts**
   Students demonstrate a sound understanding of technology concepts, systems, and operations:
   a. understand and use technology systems.
   b. select and use applications effectively and productively.
   c. troubleshoot systems and applications.
   d. transfer current knowledge to learning of new technologies.

Web Sites

Visit Ask a Tech Teacher for links and updates (http://askatechteacher.com). If you have a digital copy of this book, Ctrl+click to access links below.

1. Edutainment games and stories
2. Edutainment
3. First Thanksgiving
4. Geography game—Geospy
5. Geography—GeoNet game
6. Google Earth—free download site
7. Graphics—animated GIFs
8. Graphics—more animated GIFs
9. Graphics—even more animated GIFs
10. History—videos of events
11. How stuff works
12. Human body—body parts matching
13. Human body—the brain
14. Human Body—videos on how body parts work
15. Inventors and inventions
16. Keyboard practice—dance mat typing
17. Keyboarding—typing test
18. Mars
19. Math attack—a standard favorite
20. Math drills
21. Math edutainment
22. Math—build a bug game
23. Math/LA Videos by grade level
24. Math—quick math
25. National Gallery of Art—for kids
26. National Geographic
27. Nova video programs
28. Science headlines—audio
29. Search the internet
30. Spelling—-games to learn class words
31. Stories for all ages
32. Stories for all ages — more
33. The White House—for kids
34. Typing program—a graduated course
35. Edheads—Activate your mind

Specific to Units

Animals
Animals

Art

1. Art—Make a monster
2. Clay animations
3. Metropolitan Museum of Art
4. Minneapolis Institute of Arts
5. Mr. Picassa Head
6. Museum of Modern Art
7. National Gallery of Art—for kids
8. 50 Great Photoshop Tutorials

Cultures

1. First Thanksgiving
2. World National Anthems

Geography

1. Geography Games
2. Geography Games II
3. Geography Games III
4. States games

5. Volcano Adventure

Global Issues

Spent

Minyanland

History

1. Colonial America
2. Egyptian Madlibs
3. Egyptian Pyramids
4. Ellis Island
5. Eternal Egypt
6. Find George Washington's Portrait
7. George Washington
8. Greeks-Romans
9. Growth of the USA
10. History Central
11. History for Kids—facts, games, quotes
12. History Home on the Internet
13. Jamestown Adventure Game
14. Mt. Vernon
15. Pharaoh's Tomb Game
16. Underground Railroad
17. USA Puzzles
18. US History Map Game
19. White House

Holidays

1. Earth Day
2. Groundhog Day

Keyboarding Practice

1. Finger jig practice game
2. Free typing tutor
3. Keyboard challenge—grade level
4. Keyboard practice—quick start
5. Keyboard test—quick, adjustable
6. Keyboard—free online typing course
7. Keyboarding Fingerjig—6 minute test
8. Keyboarding for Kids
9. Keyboarding practice
10. Keyboarding resources listed
11. Keyboarding—Dance Mat Typing
12. Keyboarding—full online course
13. Keyboarding—games
14. Keyboarding—lessons
15. Keyboarding—lessons and speed quiz
16. Keyboarding—more lessons
17. Keyboarding—must sign up, but free
18. Keyboarding—quick start
19. Keyboarding—speed quiz
20. Keyboard—practice with a game
21. Krazy keyboarding for kids
22. Online practice
23. Online practice—quick start
24. Online typing course
25. Online typing lessons
26. Online typing lessons — even more
27. Online typing lessons — more
28. Typing program—a graduated course

Language Arts

1. Adjective-Noun Matching
2. Analyzing, reading and writing literature
3. Create a Wordle
4. Grammar Blast
5. Grammar Practice
6. Pickit Adjectives

Math

1. A Plus Math
2. Adding Decimals

3.   Alien Addition
4.   Angles
5.   Arithmattack
6.   Build a bug math game
7.   Count us in—variety of math practice
8.   Estimating
9.   Flashcards only
10. Game-oriented math learning
11. Interactive Math Lessons Grades 2-6
12. Learn Multiplication facts—for fun
13. Links by math topic—speed math
14. Math Basics
15. Math Basics Plus
16. Math—by Grade Level—lots of stuff
17. Math edutainment
18. Math grids—car game
19. Math links by skills
20. Math Playground
21. Math practice—requires subscription
22. Math Practice Test
23. Math practice—by skill and time
24. Math skills links
25. Math—by Grade Level
26. Math—Wild on Math—simple to use
27. Measuring angles
28. Mental Math
29. Minute Math
30. Mental Math Drills I
31. Minute math drills II
32. More Quick Math
33. Multiplication Tables
34. NumberNut Math Games
35. Ones, tens, hundreds
36. Pick a math category, take a quiz
37. Quick Math—by level
38. Quick Math
39. Quick Math II
40. Speed Math
41. Test Your Math
42. Timed math
43. Timed Tests
44. Times tables
45. Virtual Manipulatives, Tessellations
46. Word and logic problems

Miscellaneous

1.   All About America
2.   Congress for Kids
3.   Thinking Skills—Riddles
4.   Thinking Skills—Solve a Mystery
5.   360° views from around the world

Poetry

1.   Analyzing, reading and writing literature
2.   Favorite Poem Project
3.   Fourth Grade Poems
4.   Funny Poetry
5.   Glossary of Poetry Terms
6.   Magnetic Haiku poetry
7.   Musical poem—you write poem, add music
8.   Parts of Speech Poetry
9.   Poetry forms
10. Poetry with a Porpoise
11. Robo Poem
12. Shaped Poems—fun
13. Shel Silverstein

Research

1.   Dictionary.com
2.   Edutainment site—requires subscription
3.   General info research
4.   Great Research sites
5.   Internet research sites for kids
6.   Kids search engine for the internet
7.   libraryspot.com
8.   Math, reading, arcade edutainment
9.   National Geographic for kids
10. Nova video programs
11. Research for kids
12. World Almanac for Kids
13. School Tube—learning videos
14. Science headlines—audio
15. Thesaurus.com
16. Virtual Library

17. World Book Online

Science

1. A Collection of Virtual Field Trips
2. Breathing earth—the environment
3. Dynamic Earth—interactive
4. Earth Science Digital Library
5. Electric Circuits Game
6. Fantastic Contraption
7. Forest Life
8. Forests
9. Geology
10. Human Body Games
1. Moon—We Choose the Moon
11. Moon around
12. Nature—explore it
13. Ocean Currents—video
14. Ocean Videos
15. Ocean Waves—video
16. Ology Sites
17. Periodic Table of Videos
18. Planet in Action via Google Earth
19. Plant games
20. Satellite Fly-bys—by zip code
21. Science games
22. Science Games II
23. Science Games—Advanced
24. Science Games—Bitesize
25. Science Stuff
26. Smithsonian Museum
27. Solar System in 3D
28. Stardate Online
29. Virtual tours
30. Volcano Adventure
31. Water Cycle
32. Wonderville

Social Studies

1. States capitals
2. State capitals II
3. State capitals III
4. State Capitals IV

Spanish

1. Spanish resources
2. Spanish Stories

Technology

1. Computer basics
2. Computer Basics II
3. Computer parts
4. Computer puzzle
5. Crossword Puzzle Maker
6. Find the Technology
7. Internet Safety
8. Organize technology (drag and drop)
9. Parts of the computer
10. Videos on Computer Basics K-6
11. Who are your online friends?

Word Study

1. Dolch Site Word Activities
2. High-frequency words—hangman
3. Spelling practice—use with spelling words
4. Stories with Dolch Words
5. Visuwords
6. Vocabulary Fun
7. Word Central—from Merriam
8. Webster
9. Word Videos

For Teachers

1. Animations, assessments, charts, more
2. 10 Tech Alternatives to Book Reports
3. Children's University
4. Create a magazine cover
5. Create free activities/diagrams in Flash!
6. Creative Tools
7. Easy Techie Stuff for the Classroom
8. Easy-to-navigate collection
9. Eleven Little-known Facts
10. Environmental footprint
11. Flashcards or Worksheets
12. Google Earth Lesson Plans I
13. Google Earth Lesson Plans II
14. Google Earth in Math Curriculum
15. Glogster—posters
16. Hollywood Sq/Jeopardy Templates
17. How to Videos for Web 2.0
18. Jeopardy Games in PowerPoint
19. K-8 school-related videos. Tons of them
20. Make digital posters
21. Mapping ideas with a tag globe
22. Newspapers around the world
23. Online quizzes you create, online grades
24. Password creator
25. Posters—8x10 at a time
26. PowerPoint stuff
27. Print Large Posters in 8x10 bits
28. Print Posters One Page at a Time
29. Publish the magazines
30. Pupil Tube
31. Puzzle maker—for study guides, etc.
32. Shelfari—share books with students
33. So many Free online tools (Web 2.0)
34. Teaching vocab, prefixes/suffixes, more
35. Tools for studying writing
36. Training videos
10. Turn pictures into Videos—Easily

Index

Homework

HOMEWORK 5-1—SUBMIT VIA EMAIL

Submitted:	*5 points*
Late:	*-1*
Protocol error:	*-1*
Not submitted:	*0 points*

Send me an email from home with:
- Your name
- Your email address
- Your parents' names
- What you want to learn about computers
- What you know about computers

HOMEWORK 5-2—SUBMIT VIA EMAIL

Submitted: 5 points
Late: -1
Protocol error: -1
Not submitted: 0 points

Read the hints on this page and email your five favorites to me. These are from last year's Fifth Graders. Don't worry if you don't remember how to do bullets or columns—it's OK. Just do your best.

Hard things/Things I don't like

- Memorizing
- Publisher
- slideshow presentation
- Picking partners for projects
- Homework
- Speed quizzes
- Type to Learn

- Home row keys
- Unfreezing the computer
- Remembering how to do everything at once
- Figuring out what I did wrong
- Hardware is confusing
- What computer things are called is hard

Easy things/My Favorite things

- PowerPoint presentation
- Type to Learn
- Learning home row keys
- Speed quizzes
- SimTower
- Making Publisher books
- American Revolution project
- Email
- Reading on a website
- Doing things really fast
- Shortcuts

- Making tables, reports, posters
- All the projects
- How easy it is to delete mistakes
- Borders, clipart and page designs
- Computers make life easier
- Halloween stories
- Print Music, composing music on the computer
- Doing many activities at once
- Reviewing for quizzes

Advice

- Pick the right partner for projects
- Finish your homework on time
- Finish homework ahead of time
- Be responsible
- Keep on top of things
- Practice speed typing
- Memorize the keyboard
- Come in during recess to finish work
- The teacher doesn't bite!

- Study hard
- Study harder than you think you need to
- Think of computer as a regular grade, not an effort grade
- Listen to instructions on the rubrics
- Check online weekly for homework
- Always be positive

HOMEWORK 5-3 (submit email)

Submitted:	*5 points*
Late:	*-1*
Protocol error:	*-1*
Not submitted:	*0 points*

Complete the puzzle. Scan into your computer and email the completed puzzle to me or submit to drop box.

```
Q B M F E X X R N E T W O R K I F C S H D T P
R I M O Y O R E I X O V Y M B B L I R R M M U
F G P J T F A P E L B A T Y N M P W O D Y H X
J I R X N U B A D P E Y C E U R F P E N Y K X
E F A G X K L P K L S W T L O M N S O P R A T
B R B S X A O L Q W V I T T U D K N E N D U F
I L U K C M O L Z Q Q I O E O T Y R S N O X T
C R N X H R T A U U M C G W O S L W A H I U F
G D E T T L H W E E O U N P W I E R S R K U P
W E M S L F R T D L V M L G N I G A T I W N A
G X V Q U M T I Q E E S B K V N W S E G G M X
C T H H A E A P L N I O X E X O C X I H Q B W
I E C L F L M X U A M H R S P C M G R T Q B V
V N O T E T G N L F S P Q E Q I I U O T N B M
A S Y T D Z D I L P T P G L R O S R U C X T P
B I J A G Z G R I N O O M D N A W H S L K E U
B O Z L W N P X I R V R V N W H I G R I A M U
L N C M M T E R C L Q C V A V Y H S E C U P K
O M M E O L P A B C L F Q H F X N L T K R L C
L O N O S J M E P N O D P T W E Z X I M O A A
R T H A W W O T Q D G R O X Y R V H M E Z T B
T S G I T E E H S K R O W W N N M M I N J E S
C R U V V T A S K B A R S W N Y W E L U F U W
```

alignment, handles, print preview, AVI, protocol, back-up, icon, right-click menu, crop, jpg, synonym, ctrl, limiter, table, cursor, hyperlink, macro, task bar, default, menu bar, template, desktop, multimedia, tool bar, drill down, netiquette, wallpaper, wrap, pixels, drop-down menu, network, washout, extension, PC, worksheet, gif

HOMEWORK 5-4 (submit email)

Submitted:	*5 points*
Late:	*-1*
Protocol error:	*-1*
Not submitted:	*0 points*

1. Go onto technology class page
2. Take a screen print of 'What We Did This Week'. It can be any week available, just so I recognize it as a screen print (with the tool bars and task bar showing).
3. Copy-paste it into the body of an email and send to me

HOMEWORK 5-5—SUBMIT VIA EMAIL

Submitted:	5 points
Late:	-1
Protocol error:	-1
Not submitted:	0 points

Home Row   (asdfjkl;) 15 minutes per night for 3 nights

Place this printout next to your keyboard. Type the lines slowly and evenly, keeping your eyes on the text. Practice hitting the RETURN key without looking. DON'T CORRECT MISTAKES! You are trying to learn the keys NOT how to fix mistakes. Paste into body of email and send to me.

If it takes you shorter than 45 minutes, start over. Stop at 45 minutes.

```
1.  a;sldkfj a;sldkfj a;sldkfj a;sldkfj a;sldkfj
2.  aa ;; ss ll dd kk ff jj a;sldkfj fjdksla;
3.  asdf jkl; asdf jkl; fdsa ;lkj fdsa ;lkj
4.  aa ;; ss ll dd kk ff jj aa ff jj dd kk ss ll aa ;;

5.  aj sk dl f; aj sk dl f; ;f ld ks ja fj dk sl a;
6.  la ls ld lf ka ks kd kf ja js jd jf ;a ;s ;d ;f
7.  aj ak al a; sj sk sl s; dj dk dl d; fj fk fl f;
8.  asd fjk ;lk fds sdf kl; lkj dsa sdf kl; fds lkj

9.  as as ask ask asks asks ad ad ads ads as ask ads
10. sad sad dad dad fad fad lad lad all fall dads fads
11. all lad ask fad lass ad dad all fall ads
12. salad salsa alfalfa salad salsa alfalfa

13. as a lad; ask a dad; all fall; a sad lad;
14. a fall; a flas; all fall; all dads; ask dad;
15. a fall ad; a sad lass; as a dad; sad dad;
16. aa ;; ss ll dd kk ff jj a;sldkfj a;sldkfj
```

HOMEWORK 5-6—SUBMIT VIA EMAIL

Submitted:	*5 points*
Late:	*-1*
Protocol error:	*-1*
Not submitted:	*0 points*

IGN—15 minutes per night for 3 nights

Place this printout next to your keyboard. Type the lines, keeping your eyes on the text. Practice hitting the RETURN key without looking. DON'T CORRECT MISTAKES! You are trying to learn the keys NOT how to fix mistakes. This will increase your speed and your accuracy. Stop after 45 minutes. **If you are practicing at home regularly you should be seeing a big difference in your typing speed and accuracy.** Paste into body of email and send to me.

kit sit fit fist kid it lit hid hill fill sill
jag hag lag leg glad gas gag sag egg leg keg
nat nan den fan land hand sand fan tan than hen

tin sing kind king hint shine gain tag link
the then these this that thin than think
night sight light fight height night light
gang fang hang sang gang fang hang sang

a tall tale; a keen knight; a fine sight
he felt he needed the things at the sale
the lads asked the king at the east gate
he is a fine dad; she said he needs his kind
he had a kite; sing a little; he has a fish;

fail sail jail laid hail tail nail fail
sealing dealing keeling kneeling healing
if it is in the its a in at is it the then
is the; in the; if the; let the; see the;
fin din sin gin kin sit lit kit hit fit

HOMEWORK 5-7—HARD COPY

Submitted:	5 points
Late:	-1
Protocol error:	-1
Not submitted:	0 points

Complete crossword. Scan into your computer and submit via email or turn in hard copy.

alignment
handles
print preview
AVI
protocol
back-up
icon
right-click menu
crop
jpg
synonym
ctrl
limiter
table
cursor
hyperlink
macro
task bar
default
menu bar
template
desktop
multimedia tool
bar
drill down
netiquette
wallpaper
wrap
pixels
drop-down menu
network,
washout
extension
PC
worksheet
gif

ACROSS
2 The interconnected computers at the school
4 A keyboard shortcut that performs multiple steps
5 Picture compatible with websites
7 Small picture that opens a program
9 The one that shows if you don't select another
14 Shows where the mouse is
17 Up/to save a second copy in case the first disappears
18 How text or pictures are lined up on a page
19 To cut out unnecessary parts of a picture
20 The correct way to do something
21 Down menu/a list of choices when you use the menu bar
22 Many ways to communicate
23 The dots around a picture that allow you to resize

DOWN
1 The way text goes around a picture
3 Icons in a group that do something when clicked
6 Moving picture, very short movie
8 Words at top of page with drop-down menus
10 Bar at bottom of screen showing open programs
11 Click through multiple layers of file folders
12 To see what will print before printing
13 Links to a website
15 The three letters that follow a website address
16 Words used to refine a website search
19 Control key
20 The little boxes that make up a picture

HOMEWORK 5-8—SUBMIT VIA EMAIL

Submitted:	*5 points*
Late:	*-1*
Protocol error:	*-1*
Not submitted:	*0 points*

Place this printout next to your keyboard. Type the lines, keeping your eyes on the text. Practice hitting the RETURN key without looking. DON'T CORRECT MISTAKES! You are trying to learn the keys NOT how to fix mistakes. This will increase your speed and your accuracy. Stop after 45 minutes. **If you are practicing at home regularly you should be seeing a big difference in your typing speed and accuracy.** Paste into body of email and send to me.

```
mom mud mam jam more time mow mad met mat
bib bit bid rib bad book bob rob sob bow
cod cup cut cow can cat tack call cot cell

most meet team same mail man comb con car
cab cob crib clam much cost cast computer
beat beam bell ball bowl bad brim better

be bet cram crab cab mince crime can munch
Right now is the time to finish the job.
One of the men will be able to sing now.
Bob brought the cat and the dog to school.
She did not like to eat hamburgers with cheese.
He did bring his lunch to the game.
Where is the crab soup that he cooked.
Oscar would like his teacher to grade his test.
```

HOMEWORK 5-9—SUBMIT VIA EMAIL

Submitted:	*5 points*
Late:	*-1*
Protocol error:	*-1*
Not submitted:	*0 points*

Place this printout next to your keyboard. Type the lines, keeping your eyes on the text. Practice hitting the RETURN key without looking. DON'T CORRECT MISTAKES! You are trying to learn the keys NOT how to fix mistakes. This will increase your speed and your accuracy. Stop after 45 minutes. **If you are practicing at home regularly you should be seeing a big difference in your typing speed and accuracy.** Paste into body of email and send to me.

```
;p; ;p; ;p; ;p; ;p; ;p; ;p; ;p;  up; pop pat pen pet pot lap pal
k,k k,k k,k k,k k,k k,k k,k k,k ; kit, kid, kin, ink, rink, ring,
;A; ;A; ;A; ;S; ;D; ;F; ;W; ;E; ;R;

pep pen pet part pug pin pan pup
go, to, the, up, lap, sit, in, see,
Find Take Dear Send All We Eat Run

When the, As there, And the, For all we,
With this, Then the, There are, The past
sip sap lap lip slop plop flop flip slip

life, like, hike, sit, hit, pit, sip,
That is, He will, I do, She did, It eats,
To Ron, Ed, Sal, Fred, Don, Dan, Sal, Dean,

part past please tape trip trap,  president past pest spare parts hip ship

She is sending the letter to leon.
He did not go to the store.
Where are the notes for the test.
Let us know when the order gets here.
```

HOMEWORK 5-10—SUBMIT VIA EMAIL

Submitted:	*5 points*
Late:	*-1*
Protocol error:	*-1*
Not submitted:	*0 points*

Place this printout next to your keyboard. Type the lines, keeping your eyes on the text. Practice hitting the RETURN key without looking. DON'T CORRECT MISTAKES! You are trying to learn the keys NOT how to fix mistakes. This will increase your speed and your accuracy. Stop after 45 minutes. **If you are practicing at home regularly you should be seeing a big difference in your typing speed and accuracy.** Paste into body of email and send to me.

```
fvf fvf fvf fvf fvf fvf fvf fvf fvf
five cave give gave value ever van
aza aza aza aza aza aza aza aza aza
zap zany lazy zero zip zone zoom zest

zig zag zip zinc zone dozen graze faze
have have hive heave hover above brave
gave give have hive zoo size maze gaze
doze quiz froze frizz dive leave vase

a small car may not have as much zip.
a hive of bees came after the lazy dove.
it was a very hard quiz so he failed.
he gave me a zebra and waved goodbye.
she was very lazy and never saw the zoo.

he she it to the if or and up we can do
the where why when this that then they
if he is to do this job for us, he must.
I can use the large raft if i ask first.
They are sure that i can type fast.
```

HOMEWORK 5-11—SUBMIT VIA EMAIL

Submitted:	*5 points*
Late:	*-1*
Protocol error:	*-1*
Not submitted:	*0 points*

Place this printout next to your keyboard. Type the lines, keeping your eyes on the text. Practice hitting the RETURN key without looking. DON'T CORRECT MISTAKES! You are trying to learn the keys NOT how to fix mistakes. This will increase your speed and your accuracy. Stop after 45 minutes. **If you are practicing at home regularly you should be seeing a big difference in your typing speed and accuracy.** Paste into body of email and send to me.

juj juj juj juj juj juj juj juj juj juj juj juj juj
sws sws sws sws sws sws sws sws sws
jug run dug hug rug jut just our use sun fun
sew saw sow wet were wig win was won we

few sat was wag were fte drag wade dare date
junk use us fuss our four down town work two
had his use two who whose new now when was
week while with won will wall would want well

we are; we will; we want; we think that;
the of to and in for we that is this our
of the; in the; to the; for the; on the;
it is; with the; of our; and the; it is;
all an are at do for has he his if in it

Let her go. I will too. Ned wants one also.
I had a ft. of wire and an in. of twine.
I sang. Josh jogged. Helen did the work.
Nan went to Ohio U. J. L. was in the jet.
Kathy went to the store.

HOMEWORK 5-12—SUBMIT VIA EMAIL

Submitted:	*5 points*
Late:	*-1*
Protocol error:	*-1*
Not submitted:	*0 points*

Place this printout next to your keyboard. Type the lines, keeping your eyes on the text. Practice hitting the RETURN key without looking. DON'T CORRECT MISTAKES! You are trying to learn the keys NOT how to fix mistakes. This will increase your speed and your accuracy. Stop after 45 minutes. **If you are practicing at home regularly you should be seeing a big difference in your typing speed and accuracy.** Paste into body of email and send to me.

lol lol lol lol lol lol lol lol lol lol lol lol
lot log load hold done too to go do so of on old
gone tooth jolts fool good song sold fold told gold

frf frf frf frf frf frf frf frf frf frf frf frf frf
red rag ran far her rat tar the free jar dart dirt fir
first rake hard rail free are hare hair her red dear

aLa aLa aLa aLa aJa aJa aKa aKa aLa aLa
aHa aHa aIa aIa aOa aOa aNa aNa aNa aHa
He His Ned Nan Jan Nate Jake Is Lee Ned I Ira

note nose none done fore sore tore soar dare lone
tone gone roan thorn goat one rote fir far tar jar
for her; for those; for this; for their; for him; for the

He asked Jan to send the letter to Kari;
Here are the things that she sent to Nan;
is it to the go for he she that is the or and this these
He is; Hal sat; Nan gets; Is it; Jake is; Go to the;
I think I need an O; an H; an L; and a K;

HOMEWORK 5-13/14—SUBMIT VIA EMAIL

Submitted:	*5 points*
Late:	*-1*
Protocol error:	*-1*
Not submitted:	*0 points*

This counts as 2 homeworks, so plan on spending 90 minutes on this research.

Use the internet to research revolutions. Find interesting facts about:
- The American Revolution
- The French Revolution
- The Russian Revolution
- The Industrial Revolution

Find out the following information:
- Who was involved
- When did it occur
- What were the causes
- Where did it occur
- What were the results
- Two famous quotes

You may use:
- Your textbook
- Encyclopedias
- The internet
- Your parents

Email to me and upload the document so you can use it during technology class.

HOMEWORK 5-15—SUBMIT VIA EMAIL

Submitted:	*5 points*
Late:	*-1*
Protocol error:	*-1*
Not submitted:	*0 points*

Place this printout next to your keyboard. Type the lines, keeping your eyes on the text. Practice hitting the RETURN key without looking. DON'T CORRECT MISTAKES! You are trying to learn the keys NOT how to fix mistakes. This will increase your speed and your accuracy. Stop after 45 minutes. **If you are practicing at home regularly you should be seeing a big difference in your typing speed and accuracy.** Paste into body of email and send to me.

```
1. see lee fee dee led fed dead feed sea seas
2. had has he she dash lash hall heed hal
3. tea set let jet fat sat tell tall talk eat
4. feel keel leaf jell seal seek leased fed

5. hash heal shell sheds sashes ashes heals
6. jets least let fat east feat teak sat eat
7. task these dash steel leads teeth feet eat
8. lakes the these fee seals jest seek feats

9. seek the deal; at least ask a dad; a fast jet;
10. dad had the jet; he has a deal; the sale;
11. the last jet; see the last lad; the fast seal;
12. the teeth; these lads; a deal; these salads;
```

HOMEWORK 5-16—SUBMIT VIA EMAIL

Submitted:	5 points
Late:	-1
Protocol error:	-1
Not submitted:	0 points

Type the words below and email to me. Don't look at your fingers—practice 'touch typing'. Stop after 45 minutes.

Sad	Cat	Wax	Fun	Hat	Men	Fee	Hum
Bad	Fat	Tax	Run	Mat	Pen	See	Mum
Bar	Rat	Sea	Nun	Pat	Ten	Bet	Yum
Car	Bug	Tea	Cup	Bay	Let	Get	Dad
Far	Rug	Bed	Pup	Day	Net	Set	Had
Tar	Rag	Fed	But	Hayden	Pet	Vet	Mad
Sat	Wag	Red	Camp	Hen	Yet	Wet	Pad
Vat	Sat	Wed	Lamp	Lid	Bid	Hop	Nag
Raw	Vat	Bee	Fear	Rid	Did	Mop	Ham
Saw	Raw	Jam	Hear	Pie	Dig	Pop	Bug
Bat	Saw	Can	Near	Pie	Jig	Tot	Dug
Pan	Nap	Fan	Year	Big	Pig	Cow	Rug
Ran	Rap	Man	Sear	Cot	Wig	How	Hug
Tan	Tap	Zip	Pear	Dot	Dip	Now	Jug
Van	Zap	Lip	Wear	Hot	Rip	Wow	Bun
Cap	Fog	Kip	Jeer	Lot	Sip	Box	Fun
Lap	Hog	Fix	Fall	Not	Tip	Fox	Nun
Moo	Log	Mix	Hall	Pot	Fire	Jock	Run
Zoo	Bog	Six	Tall	Rot	Hire	Dock	Sun
Coo	Talk	Dog Oil	Wall	Put	Wire	Jump	Cup
Dish		Roil	Boil	Suit	Foil	Wish	Pup
		Rock	Sock	Bun	Soil		But
			Lock		Coil		

HOMEWORK 5-17—SUBMIT VIA EMAIL

Submitted:	*5 points*
Late:	*-1*
Protocol error:	*-1*
Not submitted:	*0 points*

Write a reflection of the project we are currently working on in computer class, or the one we just finished. Your thoughts on how important it is, how it affects you. Will you remember it?

Whatever comes to mind.

Stop after 45 minutes.

HOMEWORK 5-18—SUBMIT VIA EMAIL

Submitted:	*5 points*
Late:	*-1*
Protocol error:	*-1*
Not submitted:	*0 points*

Outline notes from one of your classes and email it to me. Use bullets or numbered list. Reference the book, the subject, the page, so I can find them. Add pictures to make it more interesting.

HOMEWORK 5-19—SUBMIT VIA EMAIL

Submitted:	*5 points*
Late:	*-1*
Protocol error:	*-1*
Not submitted:	*0 points*

Show me what you remember from last year about PowerPoint!
- Make a slideshow with 5 slides
- Add transitions
- Add animations
- Add text and pictures to each slide
- Use GIF's (moving pictures)
- Have a title slide and a 'the end' slide
- Each slide should tell me what you remember or don't remember about PowerPoint skills

Email it to me. Stop after 45 minutes.

HOMEWORK 5-20—SUBMIT VIA EMAIL

Submitted:	*5 points*
Late:	*-1*
Protocol error:	*-1*
Not submitted:	*0 points*

Type a letter to me telling me what I should tell next year's fifth graders about technology class and email it to me. Include:
- What you like about computers
- What you find difficult
- What your favorite computer activity is
- What your least favorite computer activity is
- What advice you would give incoming fifth graders to help them thrive in computer class

HOMEWORK 5-21—SUBMIT VIA EMAIL

Submitted:	*5 points*
Late:	*-1*
Protocol error:	*-1*
Not submitted:	*0 points*

Go to Google Earth. Email me five pictures of amazing places (Hoover Dam, Statue of Liberty, etc.). Add a caption, telling me what it is and what it means to you.

HOMEWORK 5-22—SUBMIT VIA EMAIL

Submitted:	*5 points*
Late:	*-1*
Protocol error:	*-1*
Not submitted:	*0 points*

1. Post a question to the Discussion Board
2. Answer someone else's question

Email me your question, the answer to your question and the answer to someone else's question

HOMEWORK 5-23—SUBMIT VIA EMAIL

Submitted:	*5 points*
Late:	*-1*
Protocol error:	*-1*
Not submitted:	*0 points*

Have your parents type a letter to me telling me what I should tell next year's fifth grade parents about technology class and email it to me. Include:

- Tips and secrets
- Things that they found out too late
- Things that should be explained earlier and aren't
- Things that are especially valuable
- What advice they would give incoming fifth grade parents to help them survive computer class

More Technology Books
for your Classroom

Name	
Address	
Email	
Phone Number	

Which book?	Price (print/ebook/Combo)	How Many?	P&H ($2.99/4.50 /bk)	Total
Kindergarten Tech Textbook	*$18.99/$14.99/$30.99*			
1st Grade Tech Textbook	*$22.99/$14.99/$32.99*			
2nd Grade Tech Textbook	*$22.99/$14.99/$32.99*			
3rd Grade Tech Textbook	*$22.99/$14.99/$32.99*			
4th Grade Tech Textbook	*$22.99/$16.99/$34.99*			
5th Grade Tech Textbook	*$22.99/$17.99/$36.99*			
6th Grade Tech Textbook	*$25.99/18.99/$38.99*			
K-6 Combo (all 7 textbooks)	*$143.97/$99.97/$219.99*			
55 Tech Projects—Volume I	*$32.99/$16.99/$47.99*			
55 Tech Projects—Volume II	*$32.99/$16.99/$47.99*			
Toolkit Combo—VI and II	*$59.99/$36.99/$85.97*			
16 Holiday Projects				
19 Posters for the Tech Lab	*$6.99 (digital only)*			
38 Web 2.0 Articles	*$2.99 (digital only)*			
	Total			

Fill out this form (prices subject to change).
Email Zeke.rowe@structuredlearning.net.
Pay via Paypal, Amazon, Google Ebooks or
pre-approved school district PO.
Questions? Contact Zeke Rowe.

Structured Learning
http://structuredlearning.net
AskaTechTeacher.com
Zeke Rowe